D0762222

Unholy Alliance

Unholy Alliance

GREECE AND MILOŠEVIĆ'S SERBIA

Takis Michas

Foreword by Michalis Papakonstantinou

Texas A&M University Press • College Station

The paper used in this book meets the minimum requirements
of the American National Standard for Permanence
of Paper for Printed Library Materials, z39.48-1984.
Binding materials have been chosen for durability.

*For a complete list of books in print in this series,
see the back of the book.*

Library of Congress Cataloging-in-Publication Data

Michas, Takis, 1948–
        Unholy alliance : Greece and Milošević's Serbia / Takis Michas.
            p. cm. – (Eastern european studies ; number fifteen)
        Includes bibliographical references and index.
        ISBN 1-58544-183-X
        1. Greece—Relations—Yugoslavia—Serbia.   2. Serbia—
Relations—Greece.   3. Nationalism—Greece.   I. Title.
        II. Eastern European studies (College Station, Tex.) ; no. 15.
        DF787.Y8 M48   2002

327.49504971'09'049—dc21   2001005497

To my colleagues

Richardo Someriti and Leonidas Chatziprodromidis

for their courage and persistence

"When I hear so many Greeks—
journalists, academics, politicians, intellectuals—
expressing their admiration for Karadžić,
what can I say? How can they consider as a hero
a criminal, somebody who bombed hospitals,
who placed snipers to kill kids on the streets?"

—Zoran Mutić, September, 1995

Contents

Illustrations

Foreword

One may agree or disagree with the views expressed by Takis Michas in *The Unholy Alliance,* but one cannot dispute his powers of observation, his diligence in the collection of evidence that supports his views, and his insightful comments.

Nor can one dispute that this is an interesting text to read. However, one is left with the impression that he wrote the book more from the viewpoint of a political philosopher than that of a political analyst; more from the viewpoint of a human rights activist and critic trying to bring justice to the side he supports than that of an objective observer.

What he writes is the truth as he sees it. But one cannot dispute that there may be a parallel truth of which he is not aware, or even an opposing truth that he fails to take into account. There is no one-and-only truth, and the objective truth is hard to find. Let me here remind you of Heinrich Heine's poem in which Satan caused a mirror (symbolizing truth) to fall from heaven to earth, where it broke into thousands of fragments. People then rushed to grab a piece and came away thinking that they possessed the whole mirror.

But the book must be read so that the reader can appreciate first of all how a conscientious journalist carries out his task, the sort of research he is obliged to undertake, and the way he reaches his conclusions—whatever those may be.

I happen to have my own views on the subject, not as the result of research, but from personal experience and from observing the events through the lenses of the Greek and Western media. I respect Mr. Michas's views, but I retain the right to disagree—something that I believe is the essence of an open society. Nevertheless, I totally agree with him concerning the dangers that threaten Greece as the result of the presence of extreme nationalistic tendencies.

I repeat: This book represents one side or one truth, if you will, of dramatic events that took place during a very stormy period and which concern everybody—including the Greeks who live in a country adjacent to the area of the conflict.

Michalis Papakonstantinou,
former Greek foreign minister
Athens, May, 2000

Series Editor's Introduction

Takis Michas has written a very significant book on a topic that has been dropped from consciousness by most people interested in the Balkan Wars of the 1990s, namely, the alliance between Greece and Serbia during those wars. It was an ambivalent alliance, and ambivalence always signals the existence of powerful yet conflicting emotions.

The ambivalence of the Serbian-Greek alliance stems from many factors. Greece is a member of NATO and the EU, hence a Western country, yet its culture is based upon the Orthodox faith, hence it is in some ways Eastern. Serbia was an ally of the West in both World Wars, yet its predominantly Orthodox faith also pushes it toward an Eastern direction. If only the ambivalence were this simple! In fact, the splits run deeper at every conceptual turn. It becomes nearly impossible to demarcate where the West ends and the East begins and to account for why this distinction is so charged with emotions. Both Greece and Serbia share a common antipathy toward Turkey, which is in some ways more Eastern than they are, but which in other ways is the most Western of Islamic countries. The West is ambivalent too, with its consistent prejudice toward the Balkans as "Europe's backyard," its racist attitude that "those people" in the Balkans are backward, prone to hatred, and emotionally unstable. Yet the West also used Greece and Serbia's domination of Yugoslavia as pro-Western bulwarks against the Eastern menace of Soviet domination and Soviet-styled Communism.

Perhaps no other book crystallizes this Western prejudice as clearly as Rebecca West's *Black Lamb and Grey Falcon*. And of course, Akbar Ahmed and other Muslim writers have written eloquently about the West's ambivalence toward Islamic culture. There is no firm ground here upon which to stand. Everything is constantly shifting, and readers on both sides of the so-called East-West border will benefit from reading Michas's book and confronting these and related issues.

For example, Michas invokes Samuel Huntington's popular book on the allegedly great cultural divide between Western and Eastern cultures, but he does not rely upon it exclusively. Huntington's conceptual scheme is useful, but simplistic. Huntington perceives black and white distinctions where he might have perceived ambivalence. The Balkan Wars of the 1990s were more than a clash of the Vatican-German-Croatian cultural alliance against the Orthodox-based alliance of Russia and Serbia. Russia acted as a broker for U.S. and NATO-based peace initiatives in Serbia, and Croatia, and Germany took in proportionately more Muslim refugees from Bosnia-Herzegovina than any other nations. Michas is right to penetrate beneath and behind these simplistic conceptual distinctions and to offer the rich details that a skilled journalist can see. His documentation from the Greek media concerning the reactions of the Greek public toward Serbian aggression is thought-provoking: Why did events (such as the shelling of Sarajevo) that seemed to provoke compassion for Muslims in the West provoke sympathy for Serbs among many Greeks?

Michas also offers one of the most penetrating analyses of the political games concerning the independence and naming of Macedonia. Again, ambivalence among all the concerned parties seems to be the key for understanding what happened. Macedonia's very name provoked emotional reactions in Greece concerning ancient Macedonia and its meaning for contemporary Greece, very much along the lines of the significance of the Battle of Kosovo—fought in 1389—for contemporary Serbia.

How can such dated events still provoke strong emotions? Michas rightly casts Slobodan Milošević's role in all this postemotional manipulation as the great exploiter of deeply held emotions on all sides. Milošević used the Battle of Kosovo as a springboard for promoting Serbian paranoia and fear, and he used the possessiveness concerning Macedonia's name to promote a planned take-over of Macedonia. But what is far more surprising is Michas's detailed analysis of Western ambivalence in these and other regards.

Thus, Michas demonstrates how Lord David Owen was apparently taken in by some of Milošević's grandstanding, and how Owen opposed America's efforts to launch NATO airstrikes early in the conflict. Milošević had this effect because he played on the myth of the Serbs as an oppressed, valiant people who were the West's allies. But the reality on the ground was that Milošević had set into motion a series of brutal wars against innocent people. That this is "obvious" only in hindsight suggests powerful, irrational forces at work even in the minds and hearts of Western diplomats.

In short, this book by Michas should begin to dispel the self-serving and false myths of the Balkans as Europe's irrational half-sister. By exposing how Western diplomats and Western policies played into the transparent efforts by Milošević to manipulate emotions, Michas invites Westerners to confront their own ambivalence.

Stjepan G. Meštrović
Series Editor

Acknowledgments

While writing this book I benefited from information, opinions, and criticism provided by many people. It is impossible to thank them all individually, however, there are several whose contributions were essential.

I am deeply grateful to Samuel Huntington, Stjepan Meštrović, Noel Malcolm, Roy Gutman, Nikos Mouzelis, and Adamantia Pollis for their very valuable comments, suggestions, and criticism of earlier drafts of this work. I benefited greatly from comments made by Terry Raphael and Michael Gonzalez about sections of the present work that originally appeared in the *Wall Street Journal Europe.* I also salute Karin Hope, Antonis Papaganids, and Stavros Petrolekas, who read sections of the manuscript with a critical yet compassionate eye. I am further indebted to my colleagues Angeliki Psara, Dimitris Psaras, Tasos Kostopoulos, Dimitris Trimis, and Teta Papadopoulou for their repeated generosity in providing me with material drawn from their own research. Special thanks are due to Andreas Christodoulidis of the Athens News Agency and Panayotis Dimitras of the Greek Monitor–Human Rights Watch for providing me with much-needed archival material.

I would also like to thank the following for at one point or another generously sharing with me their knowledge, ideas, and views regarding Greece and the Balkans: Paschalis Kitromilides, Mark Mazower, Thanos Veremis, Theodoros Couloumbis, Jacques Rupnic, Alexis Heraklides, Edward Mortimer, Richard Clogg, Anastasia Karakassidou, Christos Rozakis, Stefan Troebst, Nikiforos Diamantouros, Thanos Lipowatz, Michael Herzfeld, Sotiris Wallden, Panos Kazakos, Thanasis Platias, Niyazi Kizilyurek, Andreas Andrianopoulos, Alex Rondos, Teodor Bennakis, Helena Smith, Fred Reed, James Pettifer, Alex Tarkas, and Thanasis Papandropoulos. None, of course, are responsible for any judgments, misjudgments, or errors I have made.

Finally, I want to express my gratitude to Serapheim Fintanidis, editor in chief of the Greek daily *Eleftherotypia,* whose archives I used extensively while writing this book. My thanks also to features editor Sifis Polimilis for his extremely elastic patience.

Unholy Alliance

Introduction

The Setting

One day in April, 1993, the editor in chief of the daily financial paper I was working for at the time called me into his office and said, "I think that we have a small problem."

"What?" I replied.

"Can I ask you to stop writing your weekly column for a while?" he asked. It was obvious that he was feeling increasingly uncomfortable.

"Why?" I was flabbergasted.

"It has to do with the last column you wrote," he explained. "Something about sending money to a Muslim newspaper in Bosnia."

I still did not understand. I had written a column about the trials and tribulations of the famous Sarajevo newspaper *Oslobodjenje* at the end of which I had put a bank account number where one could send money to support it, as was done all over Europe.

"So?" I asked.

"We received a lot of phone calls that day from readers protesting the fact that we were asking them to send money to the Muslims so that they could buy arms to kill Orthodox Serbs," he continued. "Higher powers have asked me to tell you to stop writing your column until this whole thing is over."

I was speechless. I was, of course, aware that every time a journalist in Greece wrote something that was even mildly critical of the Serbs he was putting his professional career on the line. But the piece I had just written was not controversial at all. Could it be that Greece had moved so far apart from the rest of the world? What I found hardest to understand was the rationale behind the editorial policy. The conglomerate of which the newspaper constituted a small and relatively insignificant part was deeply involved in the process of "globalization." Its trading partners were American and European companies. Its economic interests lay in London and New York, not in Pale or Belgrade. Why, then, were they being so careful not to offend the latter?

One could extend the reasoning to the rest of the country. Greece was a country that, since its admission to the European Community (EC) in the late sixties, had been practically living on generous European Union handouts (approaching, according to some estimates, 6 percent of the Gross Domestic Product annually). What possibly could be the rationale behind the decision of the overwhelming majority of its population to support everything the West abhorred?

How could Greece, in the summer of 1993, welcome Radovan Karadzic with open arms while at the same time arrest the handful of people who had protested his visit? For someone like myself—who belonged to a generation brought up to believe that the "material conditions of existence" determined what was going on in the realm of "consciousness" or, alternatively, that people acted on the basis of utility-maximizing criteria—the Greek response to the recent Balkan wars was a mystery.

What seemed incomprehensible during the Bosnia and Kosovo wars was not so much that Greece sided with Serbia, but that it sided with Serbia's darkest side. What appeared irrational in the responses of the overwhelming majority of the population, the media, and the political class of the country, was not that they criticized the North Atlantic Treaty Organization (NATO) air campaigns but that they failed to exhibit concern for the crimes perpetrated by the Serbs against innocent Bosnians and Albanian Kosovars. In sum, what was noteworthy about the Greek reaction to the wars in the former Yugoslavia was the fact that the victims of Serb aggression were blocked out from the space of collective representations that defined the moral perceptions of the largest segment of Greek society.

This work grew out of my efforts to come to grips with this phenomenon. In a certain sense it can be seen as an attempt to answer the question posed by Serbian literary critic Zoran Mutić, who is also considered the "ambassador" of Greek letters in Yugoslavia because he translated all the major Greek poets and novelists into Serbo-Croatian. In an interview with the Greek left-wing daily *Eleftherotypia* in 1995, he expressed his sense of bewilderment about the feelings of admiration he encountered among Greek journalists, intellectuals, university professors, and politicians for the Serb war crimes, especially those of Radovan Karadzic: "When I hear so many Greeks—journalists, academics, politicians, intellectuals—expressing their admiration for Karadzic, what can I say? How can they consider as a hero a criminal, somebody who bombed hospitals, who placed snipers to kill kids on the streets?"[1]

Similarly, journalist Victoria Clark, in her book *Why Angels Fall,* recalls the experiences of her Serb assistant, Bogdan, who spent his holidays in Greece during the war in the former Yugoslavia: "You Serbs are doing a great job!" the locals used to tell him with a friendly slap on the back.[2]
It is this gesture of friendliness—not, of course, toward a Serb, but toward activities that normally would evoke horror irrespective of their source of origin—that I aim to analyze and comprehend.

During the last fifteen years I have worked for Greece's three major newspapers and have written extensively on Greek policies during the war in the former Yugoslavia.[3] My work gave me the opportunity to get acquainted with and listen to the views of some of the politicians who played a major role in the formation of Greek foreign policy.[4] Moreover, serving as a senior adviser in 1992 to Andreas Andrianopoulos, the minister of trade and industry, provided me with useful insights into the workings of government. Finally, my travels to Bosnia, Kosovo, and Macedonia gave me an opportunity to find out how others viewed Greece and its policies.

Let me note that the phenomena described and analyzed in this book were, from what I can judge at least, neither government led nor media initiated. The phenomenon of consistently supporting the regimes in Pale and Belgrade while at the same time turning a blind eye to the crimes perpetrated against innocent men, women, and children in Bosnia and Kosovo was, in the final analysis, a folk phenomenon. It was a bottom-up and not a top-down event. It was, as the economists would put it, "demand led." Most media people and politicians simply gave in to this overpowering popular demand.

I am fully aware that this statement flies in the face of much of the contemporary scholarship, which stresses the role of the elites in manipulating popular feelings. Nor can I substantiate it. Let us therefore simply say that it reflects the particular experiences of this author.

While I concur with those who argue that the Greek media did an extremely poor and one-sided job of covering the war in Yugoslavia, I would hasten to add that the reasons must, to a large extent, be sought in the public's responses. The issue here was not the media manipulating public opinion, but rather the public forcing the media to provide coverage of what it wanted to see or read about. The overwhelming majority of Greece's quality journalists—as a rule print journalists—had informed and balanced views.[5] Nevertheless, their influence in the formation of daily editorial policy during the wars in the former Yugoslavia proved to be minimal. They were immediately swept aside not by reactionary editors or publishers but by a public that craved stories about Vatican conspiracies, Muslim perfidy, Croatian cruelty, Serb bravery, Western hypocrisy, NATO war mongering and U.S. arrogance.

Let me stress at this point that the focus of the book is on the presentation and explanation of the perceptions, attitudes, and states of mind that formed the local Weltanschauung with regard to the war in former Yugoslavia. The emphasis is in other words on what Alexis De Tocqueville called in his famous phrase "habits of the heart" *(habitudes du coeur)*—as opposed to the "habits of the mind" *(habitudes de l'esprit)*—which he defined as "the whole moral and intellectual condition of a people."[6] This distinction does not signify the opposition of heart to mind, or of emotion to intellect. The concept of the "habits of the heart" refers to the preconscious societal consensus of what is politically relevant, as opposed to the concept of the "habits of the mind," which signifies fully elaborated political traditions and discourses.[7]

This work thus should not be seen as an analysis of the intricacies and vicissitudes of Greek foreign policy, on the interplay between foreign policy and domestic policy considerations, or on the influence of Greek-Serb economic exchanges on local media barons and policy makers. Nor should it be seen as offering new insights into the nature of terrorism in Greece or the relations of its banking sector and its leading businessmen with the Milošević regime. To the extent that all those issues are presented and described here, this is done only insofar as they constitute material manifestations of the symbolic realm, "traces" that guide the deconstruction of the broader ideological realm of cultural values, ideas, and perceptions.[8] Instead of writing a long, detailed narrative of the period, I tried to select and highlight certain periods I believe are representative of the mentalities or "habits of the heart" that dominate Greek society. Moreover, the order of exposition I follow is primarily chronological, although occasionally thematic. Thus, for example, chapter 9, which deals with the Ansanin case, belongs chronologically to the period of the Bosnia war, but thematically is a part of the policies Greece and Serbia followed toward Kosovo.

The emphasis of this book is thus not on government policies but rather on broad, sociocultural processes. In the last analysis, these may prove to be more important—at least from the viewpoint of individual freedom and dignity. The events of the last decade have demonstrated the weakness of Greek society, its vulnerability to the sirens of intolerance and willingness to fall under what Tom Nairn calls the "spell" of ethnonationalism.[9] The way a society functions is more important than the way a government does because it is the former that, in the final analysis, provides the space where the individual can seek his or her personal autonomy.

"An intolerant society," writes Sabrina Ramet, "is more threatening to the preservation of personal autonomy than an intolerant state. For in the intolerant state the individual is unfree in the political sphere but autonomous, perhaps even in some sense 'free' in the social sphere. In an intolerant society, however, the individual is unfree in society itself, and without freedom in society no constitutional provisions for the political sphere can make much difference."[10]

Samuel Huntington's *The Clash of Civilizations and the Remaking of World Order* appeared in the summer of 1996.[11] In it, Huntington argues that the main factors influencing the eruption of international conflicts and the formation of strategic alliances in the aftermath of the Cold War have been cultural or civilizational. In this emerging new order of things, the most serious causes of conflicts will not be economic or even political but cultural. Conflicts will take place between people belonging to different cultural formations.

Marshalling an impressive body of evidence, Huntington argues that ideological politics have given way to civilizational or cultural politics. This implies that alignments defined by ideology and superpower relations have given way to alignments defined by culture and civilization.[12] The ideological boundaries between countries established by the Cold War thus have given way to boundaries increasingly shaped by cultural factors.

In this new international context, nations will rally to those they perceive as sharing similar nationalist mythology, ancestry, religion or language. For Huntington, the main civilizations are the Sinic, Orthodox, Japanese, Hindu, Islamic, Western, Latin American, and African. Nowhere has this realignment process become more evident than in Europe. The line established by the Iron Curtain has been replaced by the line "separating the poles of Western Christianity on the one hand from Muslim and Orthodox peoples on the other."[13] This line dates back to the division of the Roman Empire in the fourth century and the creation of the Holy Roman Empire in the tenth

century. In the Balkans, this line coincides with the historic division between the Austro-Hungarian and Ottoman Empires.

This new state of affairs has produced substantial realignment in the
Balkans. The old ideological dividing line that placed Greece and Turkey as
members of the North Atlantic Treaty Organization (NATO) against Warsaw Pact members Bulgaria and Romania became suddenly devoid of meaning. A new line that pitted Orthodox Greece, Serbia, and Russia against
Muslim Turkey and Albania took its place.

A country whose actions in the international arena seem to exemplify
this new state of affairs in the most paradigmatic way is Greece, according to
Huntington. Yet, as Huntington points out, Greece has always constituted
an "anomaly," never having been able to adapt to the "principles and mores"
of NATO and the European Union (EU), while "its leaders often seemed to
go out of their way to deviate from Western norms and to antagonize Western governments."[14] Throughout the 1980s, Greece supported the Jaruzelski
dictatorship in Poland, refused to condemn the suppression of dissidents in
the Soviet Union and the shooting down of a Korean airliner, harbored
organizations perceived as terrorist by the West, opposed the deployment of
cruise and Pershing missiles in Europe, and so forth.

But all these instances of "anomalous" behavior pale in comparison to
the gestalt-switch that took place in Greek foreign policy after the new division of Europe along civilizational lines. A prime example of this switch was
Greek behavior during the recent conflicts in the former Yugoslavia. According to Huntington, Greek policies were markedly different from those
of its NATO and EU partners: It actively supported the Serbs, opposed any
idea of NATO military action against them, and violated the UN-imposed
oil embargo.

Greece's new behavior reflected a change in the geopolitical interests of
the country, which came increasingly to be perceived in civilizational or
cultural terms. This affected not only its relations with Serbia but also those
with Russia. With the demise of the Soviet Union and the communist threat,
Greece suddenly found it had mutual interests with Russia in opposition to
their common enemy, Turkey. That is why Greece had permitted Russia to
establish a significant presence in Cyprus and also explored with Russia the
possibility of bringing oil from the Caucasus and Central Asia to the Mediterranean through a Bulgarian-Greek pipeline bypassing Turkey and other
Muslim countries. "Overall, Greek foreign policies have assumed a heavily
orthodox orientation."[15]

The interpretation of Greece's policies in the Yugoslavia war that came to dominate serious Western media reporting focused nearly exclusively on the Orthodox Christian religion. Writing under the overpowering influence of Huntington's seminal work, most commentators tended to view Greece's re-actions in the context of a division between Eastern and Western Christendom. Thus, Misha Glenny saw in Greece's embrace of the Belgrade regime a "re-vival of Orthodox ties."[16] In a similar vein, French political analyst François Revel argued in the French weekly *Le Point* in October, 1993, that Greece identified itself with Serbs led by Slobodan Milošević and Radovan Karadzic "in the name of the Byzantine, the Greek Slav and the Christian Orthodox civilization, against Islam and against Rome."[17] Finally, French philosopher and social commentator Alain Finkielkraut saw in Greece's entanglement with the Belgrade regime an attempt to discover its Orthodox identity.[18]

However, interpretations of Greek-Serb relations that focus exclusively on the religious aspect tend to commit the same mistake with interpreta-tions of analogous phenomena in Eastern European societies. This mistake, as Ramet points out, consists in treating the religious sphere as an autono-mous part of society, existing independently of and not being influenced by events taking place in the latter.[19]

Although Huntington's "civilizational approach" opened up a new "theo-retical continent," to use Louis Althusser's favorite metaphor, some ques-tions remained unanswered.[20] If religion was such an important factor in the Greek response to the wars in the former Yugoslavia, how then could one explain Greece's strong ties with Muslim regimes like Muammar Qadhafi's Libya or the pro-Muslim Palestine Liberation Organization (PLO)? And what about Greece's antagonism toward the Republic of Macedonia, a predominantly Orthodox country?

Another fact overlooked in this context was that Greece was unique even among Orthodox countries in terms of the consistency and intensity of its attachments to Belgrade and Pale.[21]

According to Ramet, a fuller understanding of the place and function of religion in the political evolution of Eastern European societies requires a "systems approach."[22] In the case of Greece, an understanding of the vital role the Orthodox Church played in cementing and promoting Greek sup-port for the Serbs and Bosnian Serbs necessitates placing the institution of the church squarely at the center of the most political of processes: that of nation building. Here, the following aspects are of paramount importance: (1) The nature of Greek nationalism and its relation to religion, (2) the ar-ticulation of a concept of human rights in the political culture of modern Greece, and (3) the folk worldview.

In Greece, as in most of the states that emerged from the dissolution of the Ottoman and Habsburg Empires, the specific variant of nationalism that came to dominate was ethnic or cultural.[23]

As opposed to civic nationalism, where the focal point is the concept of citizenship and, by extension, civic rights and legal rules, in ethnic nationalism the focal point is the ethnos and its specific characteristics, genealogy myths, and symbols.[24] Whereas in the former the predominant discourse is that of voluntary contracts and choice, the latter is distinguished by the continuous generation of discourses of authenticity. Whereas in the former citizenship conveys the "sense of solidarity and fraternity through active social and political participation," in the latter the sense of fraternity and solidarity presupposes the sharing of similar ethnocultural markers.[25] Finally, whereas in civic nationalism citizens "can move in an out of pre-existing national space," in ethnic nationalism the individual is always the occupant of a specific national space.[26]

The main components of Greek ethnic nationalism are:

1. A genealogical myth of origin according to which the contemporary inhabitants of Greece are descended from the glorious Hellenes of classical antiquity. According to this conception—especially in its more folkish and populist variants—there exists an unbroken cultural continuity "through the ages" between classical antiquity and modern Greece. A direct cultural line connects the Homeric times with the Greek present.[27]
2. The Greek language, which again is seen as the main link uniting classical Hellas with modern Greece.
3. The Orthodox religion as embodied in the institution of the Greek Orthodox Church. According to Prof. Adamantia Pollis of the New York School of Social Research, national identity "became identical with the ethnic identity in which religion, and in particular the Eastern Orthodox one, became a basic constitutive element."[28] The Orthodox Church has been a tool of the state in promoting the cultural homogenization of the country, as was the case also in other Balkan and Eastern European states.[29]

It is perhaps worth noting that the construction of the modern Greek identity was not without problems. To the extent that the genealogy of the Greek cultural community tended to stress continuity with pagan antiquity, it had to confront the problem of the incorporation of orthodox Christianity. Marxist historian Tom Nairn points out that Greek nationalism performed "the astonishing feat" of convincing Greeks that they are descended from the ancient gods and that this state of affairs is coextensive with being an Eastern Orthodox Christian.[30]

Thus, the elements that constitute Greek national identity are ethnic. Religion, language, and shared genealogy define the Greek nation rather than universal citizenship rights. These characteristics differentiate the "authentic" Greek from the "others." The latter are thus defined as those who "lack" the attributes of Greekness *("ellinikotita")* even if they have resided in Greek territory since times immemorial.

The second element that must be noted is the historical articulation of a concept of individual rights in the political culture of the country. Understanding this articulation will allow us to account for the responses of Greek society to Serb human rights violations in Bosnia and Kosovo. One of the distinguishing features of the political culture of modern Greece is the absence of a concept of individual rights. This is usually attributed to the fact that the emergence of Greek nationalism was not accompanied by doctrines of individual rights and freedoms as it was in the West.[31] In Greece, as in the other Balkan countries, ethnic majoritarian rule was in continuous conflict with the idea of individual rights.[32]

According to Athens University professor Paschalis Kitromilides, a very important reason for the underdevelopment of a concept of rights was the influence of the Orthodox religion in the formation of Greek nationalist ideology in the nineteenth century. The reception of the ideas of the Western Enlightenment in the Balkans was very different from their reception in the West. In Scotland and North America, for example, the Enlightenment was received in an environment appropriately prepared for it by the experience of Protestantism and growing secularization. In the Balkans, on the other hand, they collided immediately with the ideology of the Eastern Orthodox Church.

Kitromilides says the preoccupation with the safeguarding of the unity and genuineness of Orthodoxy became the rallying point of a militant conservatism that rallied its forces during that period. What developed out of this confrontation of Enlightenment ideas with the Orthodox local tradition was not a liberal nationalism informed by Enlightenment values, but rather a militant nationalist ideology that incorporated into itself basic tenets of the Orthodox creed. The modernizing challenge in the Balkans consisted in the effort to incorporate into Balkan ideological structures the worldview and systems of values that defined Western liberalism. In the nineteenth century the European idea involved "the code of civil liberty as its fundamental ingredient."[33] But this challenge failed. The common element in the struggles for national independence in Greece (late 1820s), Serbia (1878), and Romania (1880s) was "the defeats of radical conceptions of liberty."[34] What thus was lost to Balkan culture in this process were two of the core ingredients of the system of values that informed the Enlightenment worldview: "the critical spirit and the moral temper of individual liberty"[35]

Others, however, explain the absence of a rights component in the country's political culture by emphasizing political factors. Of central importance in this explanatory model is the historical division between societies that emerged from the Habsburg Empire (Croatia, Czechoslovakia, etc.), and those that emerged from the Ottoman Empire (Greece, Serbia, etc.). The difference in the political organization of the two empires—absolutism in the former versus patrimonialism in the latter—set the parameters for the subsequent ideological and political evolution of the nations that emerged from them. The political legacy of countries like Greece, which emerged from a patrimonial empire, was a weak civil society. What came to dominate these societies was a conceptualization of democracy that decisively underplayed the liberal aspect, that is, the aspect related to individual rights and the rule of law.[36]

The third and final aspect that must be considered is the psychological profile of Greek nationalism. This can be elucidated by analyzing this system of ideas in the context of Ramet's topological matrix of nationalism.[37] This allows us to account for psychological phenomena such as the emotional intensity, aggression, and intolerance that characterized the popular support for the Serbs on one hand, as well as the reactions to Western intervention in Bosnia or Kosovo. Here, the focus will be on certain structural features of the folk worldview inherent in Greek ethnic nationalism—namely on what Ramet calls the "perception of the world" contained and reproduced in the nationalist Vulgata.

If the ideology of ethnic nationalism provides the overall interpretative framework for understanding the responses of Greek society to the wars in the former Yugoslavia, then Meštrović's concept of "postemotionalism" helps us to understand the tools used to mobilize, channel, and direct those responses. This concept refers to the process whereby "the culture industry markets and manipulates dead emotions from history that are selectively and synthetically attached to current events."[38]

In the case of Greece, the mechanisms of postemotionalism sometimes assumed paramount importance. When the Serbs attacked Vukovar, the Greek media kept reminding its audience about the crimes of the Ustashi during World War II. When Bosnian Serbs engaged in mass rapes in Foća, the Greek culture industry kept reminding its clients about the crimes the Turks committed against Greeks in the nineteenth century.

What must be noted at this point is that postemotionalism should not be restricted to the selective utilization of elements from the past. It may also be used to impose selective projections on future events. Thus, the massive expulsion of hundreds of thousands of Albanians from Kosovo was under-played by the Greek media industry, which instead focused on the question of the future danger posed by a greater Albania. Similarly, when Ratko Mladić's armies were engaged in the biggest orgy of ethnic cleansing since World War II, the Greek culture industry headlined popular fears about possible future "problems" in Thrace, where a sizable Turkish Muslim mi-nority lives.

By thus displacing the attention from event to myth, from historiography to history, from the immediately felt horror to an ideologically/geopolitically mediated reflection, postemotionalism is able to transform the meaning of the event and incorporate it in the semantics of the dominant ideology.

This work consists of two major divisions: The descriptive part, chapters 1–6, presents some of the most important and characteristic events of the Greek responses to the war in the former Yugoslavia. In the theoretical part, chapters 7–9, the nature of these events is discussed in the more general context of ideology and institutions.

Bosnia

CHAPTER I

"United Like a Fist!"

T he Bosnian Serb capital of Pale was not the only place where the
fall of Srbrenica in July, 1995, was greeted with joy and jubilation.
More subdued, yet hardly dissimilar, were the proud feelings for
the "brave Serbs" expressed in Athens, Salonika, Larissa, and many
other Greek cities. This was a fight between *us* (the Orthodox com-
monwealth) and *them* (Muslims, Catholics, Protestants, and the West),
and *we* won.[1]

One could sense the excitement in the voices of Greek television news-
casters as they reported the "fall" of Srbrenica and the "total defeat" of the
"Muslims." Their excitement was understandable. After all, this victory was
a combined Greek-Serbian achievement, epitomized, according to media
reports, by hoisting the Greek flag alongside Serbia's in defeated Srbrenica.
Placed there by Greek paramilitaries who were fighting alongside the Bosnian
Serbs, this surreal scene underlined the fact that there existed a single country in the European Union that did not share the same perceptions with the
West concerning the conflict in Bosnia.

The same night the Bosnian village fell, the Greek national television
station MEGA conducted a telephone interview with a brave Greek from
Srbrenica: "After the artillery stopped its bombardment we moved in and
'cleaned up' the place!" he informed the audience, his voice trembling from
excitement.

According to the Greek daily *Ethnos,* four flags were raised in the ruins of
Srbrenica's Orthodox Church: the Serb, the Greek, that of Vergina, and that
of Byzantium.

"They are flying now side by side," reported *Ethnos,* "a living proof of the love and solidarity of the two peoples and of the gratitude which the Serb soldiers feel for the help from the Greek volunteers who are fighting on their side."[2]

The Greek paramilitaries and Serbs who fought there together celebrated the withdrawal of UN forces, which in effect gave the victors total control of the city. Left behind unprotected were women, children, and elderly Bosnian Muslims. The Greek volunteers fought hard in Srbrenica, and three were wounded in the process.[3] They thus had every reason to celebrate. After the victory, the Greek fighters raised the flags and sang the national anthems of the two countries at the top of their voices.[4]

Formed in March, 1995, at the request of Gen. Ratko Mladić, the "Greek Volunteer Guard"—sporting as its insignia a white double-headed eagle on a black background—quickly became a regular fighting unit. Four of its members were decorated with the medal of the "White Eagle" by Radovan Karadžić in September, 1995.[5] A total of one hundred Greeks fought with the Serbs, and their main camp was in Vlasenica near Tuzla. According to spokesman George Mouratidis, the force was fully integrated into the Army of the Republika Srpska and led by Serb officers.[6] By 1996, stories about the Greek volunteers commanded one- and two-page spreads in major Greek newspapers. At the same time, some of the men became frequent guests on television talk shows. The Greek public seemed mesmerized by their stories of the hardships of military life, the danger involved in fighting the "insidious" Muslims, and the bravery of their Serb "brethren."

When the newspaper *Ethnos* ran a two-page spread about their heroic exploits in Srbrenica and elsewhere in August, 1995, the popular response was overwhelming. "Our telephone lines," wrote an editor the next day, "were constantly busy from the calls of scores of youths who were asking for information concerning the Greek force that was fighting together with the Serbs."[7]

What were these brave lads fighting for? Definitely not money; it was ideology that drew them to the battle zone. "Our religion" was the most frequent answer they gave when asked about their motives. "I am an Orthodox and I must help my Serb brethren against the Muslims," said twenty-four-year-old Vagelis Koutakos.[8] Some attributed their service to geopolitics: "I gave my blood to fight the Muslim arc," said Trifon Vasiliadis.[9] Others had still grander visions: "We are fighting for a Greater Greece in a Europe free from Muslims and Zionists," proclaimed Apostolos Bambos in a television interview.[10] By fighting with the Serbs they were, in effect, fighting for the defense of their own Fatherland: "The Vatican, the Zionists, the Germans and the Americans conspire against the Orthodox nations. Their next target after Serbia will be Greece!" exclaimed volunteer Spiros Tzanopoulos.[11]

If they felt any sorrow for the slaughtered men, women, and children they must have stumbled upon in their fight for country and religion, they did not show it. But then, few of their countrymen back home showed any signs of remorse for those who were displaced, raped, or killed in Bosnia. Indeed, throughout the war there, not a single major Greek political party; not a single prominent Greek politician, businessman, priest, artist, film director, author, or trade unionist—in other words, not a single public figure of any renown—had the courage, the will, or the inclination to stand up and publicly condemn the shelling of Sarajevo or the Serb atrocities in Srbrenica, Foća, Zvornik, or anywhere else for that matter. Whereas many public events were organized in solidarity with the suffering Serbs, not a single public event was staged to protest the murderous ethnic cleansing by the Serbs in Bosnia and elsewhere.

An example of the selective sensitivities exhibited by Greek artists were the concerts Greek singers organized in Belgrade to express their solidarity with the Serb war effort. Two such concerts were particularly important. The first, held December 12, 1992, was sponsored by the Greek-Serb Friendship Association. This concert featured popular Greek singers Maria Dimitriadi and Kostas Thomaidis.[12] The second concert was held on June 30, 1994, at the Sava Center in Belgrade. It featured the extremely popular Greek singer Giorgos Dalaras. The next day, Minister of Culture Nanta Popova Pertsits invited Dalaras to the ministry to congratulate him.[13]

Throughout Karadžić's five-year effort to seize Sarajevo, not a single Greek artist or musician visited the city to express solidarity with a people who had come to represent in the West the symbol of the fight against the terror of forced ethnic homogenization. In fact, the overwhelming majority of Greek political, cultural, and business elites carefully refrained from publicly voicing anything that could be construed as even a mild criticism of Serbian human rights violations.

Whenever a Greek politician voiced criticism during the war in Bosnia it was, in most cases, directed against the occasional NATO air strike and the machinations of the West. It was the West, after all, which according to local perceptions had been responsible for the mayhem in the former Yugoslavia. Even as late as April, 1994, when the Serb atrocities had been established beyond any reasonable doubt, the only critical remarks Prime Minister Andreas Papandreou made when he met with Vladislav Jovanović, foreign minister of the Former Republic of Yugoslavia (FRY), in Athens in April,

1994, were directed against NATO "for the policies it follows in Bosnia." As far as the Yugoslav official was concerned, "the Greek and the Serb people are united like a fist."[14]

Throughout the recent war in the Balkans, Athens and Belgrade were indeed united, as Jovanović put it, "like a fist." Those ties were a reality and they operated on all levels, although they were never formalized in a treaty or military alliance. Only once did the question of formalizing those ties appear as a real and imminent option. That happened in December, 1994, when Serbian president Slobodan Milošević proposed, during one of his visits to Athens, the creation of a confederation between Greece and Serbia that would also include the Former Yugoslav Republic of Macedonia (FYROM). The Greek government's reaction to Milošević's proposal was positive—at least in words. Prime Minister Papandreou declared his support in principle for the proposal during a press conference: "We think that the proposal is a pioneering and interesting one which however we have not examined yet."[15]

Papandreou, like Constantine Mitsotakis before him, was an admirer of the Serb president and never made any effort to hide it. He was always full of praise for Milošević, whom he considered "a man of peace who plays the most important role in the pacification of the region."[16]

George Mangakis, who a few months later became the Greek deputy foreign minister, was even more enthusiastic about Milošević's proposal. He saw it as a step in the formation of an Orthodox alliance—an "orthodox arc" as it was called—that would effectively protect Greece's national interests from the "insidious powers" promoting Turkish and Muslim interests in Europe.[17]

However, the net result of Milošević's proposal was a serious rift in the pro-Serb policies of the Greek political establishment. A very strong reaction came from the aging conservative Greek president, Constantine Karamanlis. It took the form of leaks by "anonymous sources close to the president" who characterized Milošević's proposal as "unrealistic" and "dangerous." Although it would do nothing more than provide a formal mantle to an already existing state of affairs, its acceptance would almost certainly get Greece into serious trouble with its allies in NATO and the European Community. President Karamanlis, who had had been one of the main protagonists of Greece's entry into the EU, would never allow that to happen, so the proposal was subsequently shelved.[18]

The attitude of turning a deaf ear to Serb human rights violations also characterized the Greek Orthodox Church's reaction. "The Orthodox Church is on the side of the Orthodox Serb people," declared Archbishop Serapheim in May, 1993.[19] A year later, when no one doubted that the Serbs were committing massive crimes in Bosnia, the Orthodox Church leader reiterated his denomination's unconditional support for its Orthodox brethren: "Greece should always keep in mind that our natural ally is Serbia." He argued that the nation's history, tradition, and ties to Serbia should determine Greece's foreign policy—even if it conflicted with the policy of Greece's European allies.[20]

The attitude of the Greek Orthodox Church was understandable. Having been one of the most ardent supporters of the military junta that ruled Greece from 1967 to 1974, it relished its newfound role as the vanguard of this epic "clash of civilizations."[21] Not only did the church abstain from criticizing Serb atrocities, some of its clergy also traveled regularly to war-ravaged Bosnia to provide spiritual succor to the Bosnian Serb army and to conduct church services with Serb priests in the presence of Serb officers.[22] They also visited Serb army barracks, prayed with the soldiers for final victory, and posed with them for pictures that were widely distributed in Serbia.

Such was the case with a delegation from the Greek Church that visited the Serb side of Sarajevo in early February, 1995. Led by Archimandrite Ignatios of the Diocese of Piraeus, representatives of the Greek Church met with Radovan Karadžić and visited and gave their blessings to Serb troops who had been shelling the Bosnian capital daily since April, 1992. The troops' efforts resulted in the death of twelve thousand civilians, including seventeen hundred children. However, there was not a single mention of those tragic events in the report of the priests' visit that appeared in a monthly journal published by the Diocese of Piraeus. On the contrary, the report was full of praise for the "brave Serbs soldiers, the best in the world" who "are struggling and sacrificing themselves for their faith and their country."[23]

Occasionally Greek Orthodox priests would visit the sites of ethnic cleansing and other crimes committed against Bosnians and perform church services with their Serb brethren. Such was the case in December, 1993, when a delegation of Greek Orthodox priests from Salonika visited the Bosnian city of Zvornik. There, together with Bishop Basil of the Serb church, they conducted the Christmas liturgy in the church of Saint Nikolas, the protector of Zvornik.[24] A year earlier, a paramilitary unit known as the "Tigers," led by Serb warlord Arkan, engaged in indiscriminate killings and other human rights violations while "cleansing" Zvornik of its Muslim population. José

1. "They raised the Greek flag in Srebrenica." Photo from Srebrenica *by Antixcholia (Athens: Carthago, 1999).*

Maria Mendiluce, the most senior official from the office of the United Nations High Commissioner for Refugees (UNHCR) in the former Yugoslavia, who was passing through Zvornik the day it fell, said he "was detained for two hours before I realized that I was at serious risk. I could see trucks full of dead bodies. I could see militiamen taking more corpses of children, women, and old people from their houses and putting them on trucks. I saw at least four or five trucks full of corpses. When I arrived the cleansing had been done. There were no people in the streets. It was all finished"[25]

In January, 1995, the municipality of Kalamaria in Salonika declared itself a sister city to Zvornik. By that time Zvornik had been thoroughly "cleansed" of its Muslim population.[26] However, the event that defined in the most characteristic way the nature of relations between Greek political and religious leaders on one hand and Serb war leaders on the other, was the open-air mass meeting organized in Piraeus Stadium in the summer of 1993 to honor Radovan Karadžić. Invited personally by Archbishop Serapheim, Karadžić met formally with Prime Minister Constantine Mitsotakis, who at the time was the leader of the conservative New Democracy Party. He also met with Andreas Papandreou, leader of the socialist PASOK Party.

What was especially noteworthy about the event was the fact that the Greek Orthodox Church organized it.[27] This went far beyond the church's usual expressions of solidarity with the Serb Orthodox Church and the Serb people. Inviting the Serb warlord to Greece and staging celebrations in his honor were not religious acts. They were purely political acts signifying, in effect, the recognition of the Republika Srpska as a legitimate political entity with Karadžić as its prime minister. Even more serious were the moral implications of this act. The identification of the Greek Church with the Bosnian Serb leader meant the endorsement of the politics of ethnic cleansing directed against the Bosnian Muslim civilian population, as well as the practice of shelling Sarajevo daily.

The support and endorsement of Karadžić's policies by the Greek Orthodox Church was also evident in statements made after the meeting between the Bosnian Serb leader and the head of the Greek Church. "I have to stress that both the Greek and the Serbian churches are deeply patriotic," Karadzic told Archbishop Serapheim, who replied that the Greek people were watching the Serbs' struggle with great interest and were on their side. "The Greek Church," he added, "cannot but support together with the Greek

2. Radovan Karadžić awarding the medal of the "White Eagle" to Greek paramilitaries in September, 1995. Photo from the author's private archive.

people the struggle of the Serbs."[28] The Greek-Serb Friendship Association and its president, Aris Mousionis, were also instrumental in bringing Karadžić to Greece. Formed in 1992, this group played a pivotal role in propagating the Serb view during the wars in the former Yugoslavia. Mousionis, who was present at the meeting between the Greek Orthodox prelate and the Bosnian Serb warlord, told me some years later that Archbishop Serapheim "was ecstatic at having met Karadžić. At one point in the meeting Karadžić tried to kiss the archbishop's hand, but the latter pushed him gently away saying, 'It is I who must kiss your feet!'"[29]

Aris Mousionis was also present in the meeting between Karadžić and PASOK leader Andreas Papandreou, who a few months later again became the Greek prime minister. "Papandreou was a great admirer of Karadžić," he later told me. "However, he was not very knowledgeable about what was going on in the war in Bosnia nor did he have any historical knowledge of Yugoslavia and the crisis. It is indicative of his ignorance that throughout the meeting he kept calling Karadžić "Comrade," as if the latter were a communist partisan!" According to Mousionis, Papandreou's warm support for the Bosnian Serbs derived primarily from his irritation concerning the West's lack of support for the Greek claims vis-à-vis Turkey and Macedonia.

3. *Bosnian Serb leader Radovan Karadžić meets with Greek prime minister Constantine Mitsotakis in Athens in the summer of 1993. Photo courtesy Dimis Argyropoulos.*

4. *Bosnian Serb leader Radovan Karadžić together with Greek PASOK leader Andreas Papandreou in Athens in the summer of 1993. In the middle is Aris Mousionis, Papandreou's personal intermediary with Karadžić and Milošević. Photo courtesy Dimis Argyropoulos.*

5. *Radovan Karadžić embraces a member of a Greek folk-dancing group during a celebration honoring the Bosnian Serb leader staged in the Piraeus stadium "Irinis Kai Filias" in the summer of 1993. Photo courtesy Dimis Argyropoulos.*

6. "We have with us God and the Greeks," Radovan Karadžić tells a cheering crowd during a celebration honoring him in the summer of 1993. Photo courtesy Dimis Argyropoulos.

Apart from the Greek Orthodox Church, which was the main organizer of the festivities honoring Karadžić, leading Greek politicians representing the nation's entire political spectrum also took part. There to honor the Bosnian Serb leader were Kostas Karamanlis, leader of the New Democracy Party, and Minister of Defense Akis Tsochatzopoulos of the PASOK Party, as well as leading politicians from the smaller parties. In response to the thunderous applause of the masses of people who had come to see him, Karadžić declared: "Everybody is telling us to lay down our arms because we are alone. We say no, we are not alone. We have with us God and the Greeks."[30] Taking the floor after the Serb leader, the representative of the Greek Orthodox Church replied: "Greece is on the side of its Orthodox Serb brethren who are suffering trials and humiliations. We have a holy duty to help our brethren to face this ordeal"[31]

What was interesting about this event was not only the fact that official Greece—its church, political class, trade unions, and so forth—organized festivities for someone suspected of being responsible for serious crimes, but also that the Greek state forcibly tried to keep citizens from protesting Karadžić's presence. The same day the festivities were being held, four members of the small Maoist group OAKKE were arrested by police in Athens for putting up posters that read: "Throw the butcher Karadžić out of Greece."[32]

This political group, consisting of just a handful of people, was the only force that tried to stage a public protest during the Serb warlord's visit.

But the honors that Greece bestowed on Karadžić, did not end with these celebrations. In August the municipality of the island of Zakinthos decided to make the Bosnian leader an honorary citizen of the community. This event was to take place in the context of the celebrations for the protector of the island, Saint Dionisius.[33] The decision by a municipality of no particular political or economic importance was significant in that it showed the spontaneous feelings of approval, if not adoration, for Radovan Karadžić that existed throughout the country. In fact, none of the events honoring Karadžić evoked negative reactions other than those of a handful of intellectuals and journalists who had adopted dissenting positions at the very outset of war in the former Yugoslavia. They were considered natural expressions of the solidarity Greek citizens were supposed to feel and show for their fellow Orthodox Christians.

However, outside Greece the activities raised a storm of protest. Especially strong were the protests organized in Germany by the "Society of

7. *Bosnian Serb leader Radovan Karadžić meets with Archbishop Serapheim of the Greek Orthodox Church. Photo courtesy* Eurokinisi.

Threatened Peoples" and its leader, Tilman Zuelch, who had taken a very active part in past demonstrations against the military dictatorship that ruled Greece from 1967 to 1974. He had also organized protests against the Turkish invasion and occupation of the northern part of Cyprus in 1974. In that sense, he could by no means be accused of harboring anti-Greek feelings.

In March, 1994, Zuelch, together with thirty Bosnians and some German women, occupied the Greek section of the International Tourist Fair in Berlin. The occupiers raised a banner that read: "Greece supports Serb war criminals." He explained the reasons for the action in an interview with a Greek newspaper: "We are protesting about Bosnia. We accuse Greece for cooperating with the Serb government in order to annihilate the Bosnians." According to Zuelch, Greece, by supplying the Serb war machine with petroleum products from Salonika, was violating the international embargo. Moreover, war criminals like Milošević and Karadžić were being treated like heroes in Greece.[34]

Radovan Karadžić next visited Greece at the end of January, 1994, when he met with Andreas Papandreou—who had again become prime minister. He also met with Foreign Minister Karolos Papoulias. The official reason for his visit was to attend a medical conference on "The effects of the embargo and the war on the health of the Serb people."[35]

What the Bosnian Serb leader enjoyed most about Greece was visiting the little harbor near Piraeus formerly known as Turkolimano ("the harbor of the Turk") but which had recently been linguistically "cleansed" and renamed Mikrolimano ("the small harbor"). There he would sit, sipping ouzo while regaling the company of intellectuals, journalists, and politicians who had gathered to see him with stories about the unjust war the "foreigners" had imposed upon his country.

"Passersby taking their stroll this warm summer night," read a typical newspaper report of Karadžić's outings, "would stop to shake hands with the Serb leader. The fact that they could not speak his language did not seem to matter. The warm handshake, the expressions in their eyes, were enough to express their solidarity."[36]

Karadžić came and went. And so did Milošević, who visited Greece in January and April, 1991, and March, 1992. The above, of course, refer only to official visits made by the two leaders.[37] One can only speculate on their reputed incognito visits. Other dignitaries from Belgrade and Pale regime visited Greece during this period as guests of the Greek government, the church, trade unions, political parties, and student unions. Those official invitations rarely included members of the hard-pressed antiwar opposition in Serbia, and never, of course, any Bosnians. "The Greek Embassy in Belgrade was unwilling to grant visas to members of the Serb democratic opposition," said Milan Protić, a leading figure in the opposition. "We never felt welcome in the Greek Embassy." Protić became mayor of Belgrade after Milošević's fall in October, 2000.[38] For the majority of Greeks, the only Serbia that existed was that of Milošević, Karadžić, and Mladić.

The role of the Greek media in downplaying or even failing to report Serb atrocities cannot be underestimated. "People in Greece were not informed about the crimes committed in Bosnia," said Athanasios Papandropoulos, former president of the European Union of Journalists. "The way most media downplayed or failed to mention the horrors of Srbrenica and other sites of crimes reminds me of the way some neorevisionist historians downplayed or denied the existence of Auschwitz."[39]

Throughout the war in the former Yugoslavia one would have been hard-pressed to find mention in a Greek newspaper of a single editorial condemning the crimes against the Bosnian Muslims. Moreover, reports of Serb atrocities by the United Nations, Amnesty International, Human Rights Watch, and others would rarely command more than a few lines in the inside pages of most newspapers—and then only to be dismissed as part of the Western "propaganda campaign" aimed at discrediting Orthodoxy.

On the contrary, what one found was a steady diet of horrid Muslim atrocities. Let us consider the four-month period September through December, 1992. In September, the Greek people were informed that basements in Sarajevo had been transformed into torture chambers in which more than ten thousand Serbs were being maltreated. The news in October concerned two poor Serbs who had been roasted alive after being tied on a spit by evil Muslims. That same month, the Greek public was horrified to hear that the Bosnians were getting ready to use deadly toxic gases against advancing Serb forces. In December, Greek readers saw pictures of Muslims posing with big grins on their faces while holding in their hands the heads of three decapitated Serbs.[40]

The war in Bosnia was covered almost exclusively by correspondents reporting from Pale, Belgrade, or the Serb part of Sarajevo. Not a single Greek journalist was accredited by the legal government of Bosnia-Herzegovina. Nor was a single Greek journalist based in the *real* Sarajevo during the war. This meant, Ios pointed out, that the totality of the reporting in Greece from the war originated from the Serb side of the war front. As a result, Ios concluded, "the reporting reproduced to a large extent the Serb view of events."[41] Although Greek correspondents covered the expulsion of Krajina

Serbs in the minutest detail, no Greek news organization deemed it worthwhile to send its journalists to cover the horrors of Srbrenica, Goražde, Foća, Žepa, or the concentration camps.

Throughout this period, three things stand out that were emblematic for the questionable nature of the media coverage of the war. The first was the fact that war reporting was in most cases filtered through incessant pro-Serb editorializing. The second concerned the coverage of the daily shelling of Sarajevo. Whenever they were reporting the news from Sarajevo, one journalist noted, the majority of the Greek media always omitted two very central facts: "That the victims in most cases were unarmed civilian residents of Sarajevo and that the killers are in most cases Serb nationalist paramilitaries (Chetniks) that occupy the surrounding hills."[42] The third characteristic of media manipulation consisted of showing the horrors committed by the Serbs but then attributing them directly or indirectly to the Croats or Muslims.

One such case happened during a visit to the destroyed city of Vukovar organized by the Serbs for the benefit of some Greek journalists. In most of the stories that appeared in the Greek press reporting the visit, one could hardly find a single line indicating that it was the Serbs that had caused the massive destruction. Indeed, the impression the reader was bound to form in many cases was that the Croatians had bombed themselves![43]

A similar event occurred on June 19, 1995, during a broadcast of the state-run television channel ET-2. That evening, the station aired a French documentary on the tragedy of Sarajevo. However, the station followed up this excellent documentary with telephone calls to viewers asking them to contribute money to a bank account belonging to the Greek-Serb Friendship Association, the chief promoter of Serb views in Greece!

Leonida Chatziprodromidi, the leading Greek analyst of the war in the Balkans, says that the Greek media in many cases consciously engaged in what Stjepan Meštrović calls "postemotionalism." According to Chatziprodromidis, "The Greek media tried not to see what was actually happening by escaping into the past, into history, into the myths they were creating in order to justify or hide the crimes."[44]

Take the seizure of Vukovar. During the Yugoslav army's three-month bombardment of that city, the Greek media kept informing its audience about the massacres the Ustashi had committed in 1941. Another example is the events in Bosnia. While the forces of Mladić, Šešelj, and Arkan were killing innocent civilians in Bijeljina, Brcko, Zvornik, Foća, Prijedor and many other places in Bosnia, the Greek media kept describing events as the "advance of the Serb army" and reminding their audience about the proud partisan tradition of the Serbs and their fight against the Nazis during World War II.[45]

The majority of Greek reporters were more interested in presenting the views of the Belgrade regime than the actual events. This opinion was shared by Serb opposition figures. "We learned much more about the activities of the Milošević regime from the media in the West than from the Greek media," said Saša Mirković, vice president of radio station B92.[46] Zoran Mutić, a Serb intellectual and translator of Greek literature in Serbo-Croatian, was even more blunt in his assessment of the situation: "The Greek media are carrying out a naive pro-Serb disinformation campaign. In no other country in the world has something similar happened."[47]

What was equally distressing was the fact that the Greek media unwittingly became part of the power struggle that was going on in Belgrade. Serb authorities were using pro-Milošević articles written in the Greek press in their fight against the Serb democratic opposition. According to Petar Luković, who at the time was deputy editor of the Belgrade weekly opposition paper *Vreme,* the Milošević regime was "using the Greek media in order to strengthen its power."[48]

One of the worst cases of misuse of the Greek media by the Milošević regime happened in the early 1990s when a Greek weekly published a European Community document stating the names of Serb opposition political organizations that were being financed by Brussels. For Saša Mirković, "this act constituted one of the most serious and dangerous attempts at undermining the efforts of the Serb opposition by presenting its members as being in the payroll of foreign powers." An attitude of neglect verging on contempt characterized relations between the Greek government and the independent media in Belgrade. "The Greek governments," added Mirković, "refused to recognize the role of the independent media in Serbia. They did not know and they did not want to know what was happening in our country."[49]

Of course, not everybody shared those negative feelings about the Greek media's coverage of the war. The Serb authorities were thrilled and would go out of their way to praise Greek reporters for their "constructive" and "objective" accounts of events. "The Greek journalists," said Press Minister Pavlović in March, 1993, "showed great strength in resisting the false accusations against the Serb people and Serbia that are being fabricated abroad." He added that Greek journalists could be counted on to objectively report the facts.[50] Serb warlords were equally grateful for the role of the Greek media. "I want to thank the Greek press for their support," warlord Arkan told a group of Greek journalists visiting him in Bosnia in 1993.[51]

In some cases, Greek officials reportedly tried to prevent Western journalists based in Greece from contacting Muslims in "ethnically cleansed" areas in Bosnia. This was the case with Dutch journalist Ingeborg Beugel, who in the fall of 1994 traveled with a Greek humanitarian aid convoy whose destination was, as was nearly always the case, the Bosnian Serbs. The convoy was organized by Greek trade unions and its destinations were Banja Luka and Doboj. As she reported in the Dutch weekly *Elsevier* and in her radio news program in Amsterdam, Greek officials physically prevented her from talking with Muslims who were too old or too sick to leave the area. "When I tried to talk to a Muslim family in a Red Cross Center, the Greek organizer grabbed my tape recorder and pulled me forcibly out of the room while shouting: 'Don't you know that you should not be talking to them!'"[52]

The Greek-Serb Friendship Association and its president, Aris Mousionis, organized many of the visits to Bosnia's ethnically cleansed sites by Greek journalists. In the spring of 2001, when I asked him why Greek reporters never mentioned the fate of the Bosnians, he said: "The media wanted stories of Serb bravery not of Muslim suffering. We were only too happy to oblige. As for the journalists, they were behaving in exactly the same way as the rest of the Greek population."

Throughout the war in Bosnia, the Serb propaganda machine exploited the traditional fears and prejudices the majority of Greeks entertained about Turkey.[53] Thus, in their interviews and statements to the Greek media, Serb dignitaries would repeat the same message: Greece is facing a Turkish-Muslim threat; a Muslim arc is encircling Greece. This message soon achieved the status of a mantra in Greek public discourse as the media conjured up a powerful picture of bloodstained mujahideen of preferably Turkish descent ready to swarm into Greece.[54]

Slobodan Milošević was one of the first to realize the powerful appeal this message would have on the Greek psyche. On his visit to Greece on March 16, 1991—just before he ordered the attack on Bosnia—he declared that "the spirit that united us during the period of Turkish rule" once again united Greeks and Serbs. It is noteworthy that he made this statement during his visit to the Holy Mount of Athos, a major center of the Eastern Orthodox spiritual tradition.[55]

The message of the common Turkish-Muslim threat the two nations faced was cleverly reinforced by various Serb leaders during the frequent interviews they gave to a Greek media only too eager to publish them. In 1996, General Mladić told journalist Theodoros Rousopoulos that if war broke out between the Greeks and Turks, Greece could count on having "50,000 Serbs on her side."[56] In a similar vein, Radovan Karadzic declared in front of a Greek delegation visiting Pale that the Serbs would fight on the side of the Greeks if the latter were to face a Turkish attack.[57] On another occasion, the Bosnian Serb leader stressed that he was in contact with members of the Kurdish national patriotic movement, who were " fighting for their freedom."[58]

"In Bosnia, 10,000 Turks are fighting on the side of the Bosnian Muslims," warlord Arkan told another interviewer. "We must bring about the union of all the Orthodox peoples. It is not only Serbia that is threatened by Turkey but also Greece."[59]

Sometimes Serb officials went so far as to claim that they were fighting the Bosnians because they wanted to protect Greece. This was the case with the "defense minister" of the Serb Republic, Dušan Kovačević, who stated that the war in Bosnia stemmed from the fact "that the Turks want to encircle Greece through the creation of a Muslim state in the area with the intention of isolating Greece from its Orthodox neighbors."[60] The Serb leaders were also adept at exploiting the Greek Orthodox penchant for conspiracy theories. One of the most talented in this respect was Radovan Karadžić, who in February, 1992, revealed a "satanic" German plan to colonize Bosnia with Turkish immigrants from Germany in an effort to facilitate the spread of Islam throughout the Balkans.[61] He also thanked the Greek journalists interviewing him for their support.

Occasionally racial arguments were advanced in an effort to promote Greek-Serb unity. In December, 1993, Dušan Kanazir, a member of the Serb Academy of Science, told a Greek audience that they "and the Serbs share a common genetic inheritance." The only reaction to this statement came from the Athens Academy and the Greek Ministry of Foreign Affairs, which decorated him for it.[62]

The Serbs' unparalleled sophistication in trying to sell their message to the Greeks was matched only by the latter's occasionally impressive naiveté and inability to see through the Serb gimmicks. The following incident is indicative of this state of affairs. According to reports in the Greek media, members of a team of Greek actors visiting the Serb-occupied part of Sarajevo were particularly impressed by indicted war criminal Ratko Mladić, who gave them a welcoming speech. What impressed them most, they declared afterward, was Mladić's knowledge of classical Greece.[63]

The constant repetition of the theme of the "Muslim threat" repeated in innumerable articles in Greek newspapers was extremely effective. It thus was not surprising that the majority of the Greek population looked favorably upon Serb attempts to eliminate this "threat" in Bosnia. A May, 1994, poll showed that 72 percent of Greeks (as opposed to the European average of 32 percent) favored the withdrawal of "foreign [peacekeeping] forces" from Bosnia. The consequence of such a move would have been the annihilation of the seriously underarmed Bosnian Muslims. It is perhaps worth noting that there were no Greek troops in Bosnia at the time, so it cannot be argued that the poll expressed a desire to bring home Greek soldiers.

"From the moment the Bosnian Muslims were demonized by the mass media, the church and the politicians as being 'infidels,' 'friends of the Turks,' [and] 'Muslims'," explained Ilias Katsoulis, a political science professor at Panteion University in Athens, "every crime committed against them was justified in the eyes of the average Greek."[64]

The same attitude was reflected in the humanitarian assistance Greece was providing to the war-torn region. Despite the fact that the ethnic group that suffered most in the war was the Bosnian Muslims, they received little of the semiofficial Greek aid to the former Yugoslavia. The final destination of nearly all the humanitarian convoys starting from Greece was either Serbia or Serb-held areas in Bosnia, where the shipments ended up in the hands of the Serbs—or rather in the hands of the local Mafia, which had the first say in the way the food was distributed.[65]

Moreover, the Greek government was also accused of reneging on its 1993 promise to the UNHCR to accept 150 former inmates of Bosnian concentration camps. It did this by imposing conditions that disqualified Bosnian Muslims. A representative from the UNHCR said that they believed "Greece placed those terms on purpose to avoid having Muslim refugees." Greek authorities denied the allegation.[66]

Perhaps the saddest aspect of the anti-Muslim prejudice was the "ethnic filtering" Greek authorities employed when they invited children from Bosnia to visit Greece as a humanitarian gesture. In almost all cases, the so-called Bosnian children turned out to be ethnic Serbs, in many cases not even from Bosnia.[67]

It may be of some interest to note that the anti-Muslim fears did not abate—even after the Dayton agreements. At that time they were being fueled by secret intelligence reports that were being "leaked" to the media. These reports predicted attacks by ferocious Islamic mujahideen against the Greek soldiers stationed in Bosnia as part of the UN peacekeeping force

(IFOR). In February, 1996, a purportedly classified report by the Greek Intelligence Agency (EYP) "leaked" to the media stated that the Greek military
mission in Visoko would probably be attacked by Muslim forces and the act
attributed to the Serbs. This would provide the IFOR with an excuse to
intervene.[68] The attack never materialized.

But it was not only the message of the Muslim threat that helped cement
the Greek-Serb alliance. An equally powerful message concerned the threat
to the Greek Orthodox people posed by the Vatican. Some claimed that the
Pope's incessant scheming was the main factor in the dissolution of Yugoslavia and the ensuing bloodshed. Archbishop of Greece Christodoulos, who
at the time was the Bishop of Dimitrias, voiced one of the most representative expressions of this view: "We saw the Vatican siding with the international forces of Evil in order to implement the New Order of things which
prefigures Antichrist."[69]

However, representatives of Greece's established church were not the only
ones to promulgate the anti-Catholic message. The country's political leadership voiced similar views. During the period of the New Democracy government (1991–93) Deputy Defense Minister Spilios Spiliotopoulos, who
was reportedly very close to President Karamanlis, stated that the Vatican
was financing the Bosnian Muslims in their fight against the Serbs.[70] During a meeting of the Western European Union in Paris in December, 1992,
the Greek official stated that the Bank of the Vatican had given the Bosnians
$200 million, which the latter used to buy arms. This statement by the
Greek minister alarmed Greece's small Catholic community and led to strong
protests by its religious leaders.[71]

In the same vein, PASOK's deputy, George Romaios, who later became
the minister of public order, argued that the Vatican had placed its political
and economic power at the service of the Bosnian Muslims, the aim being
"the weakening of Orthodox Serbia and the strengthening of the Vatican's
role in the 'New Order' that is being planned for the Balkans."[72]

However, the most significant statement in this torrent of official anti-
Catholic discourse belonged to PASOK Party leader Andreas Papandreou.
In an analysis of the crisis in Yugoslavia published in *Ta Nea* a few months
before he again became Greece's prime minister, Papandreou laid the blame
for Yugoslavia's dissolution squarely at the feet of the Vatican and Germany,
while making no mention of Milošević's role in fermenting ethnic unrest
and nationalist feelings in his thousand-word article. The crisis in Yugoslavia, wrote Papandreou, "was nurtured by the two old friends from the Second World War: Germany and the Vatican."

Such a statement originating from the leader of an EU and NATO country was remarkable not only for its allocation of blame for the mayhem in Yugoslavia, it was also remarkable in its insinuation that the Vatican had been allied with Nazi Germany during the War World II and that the present relationship between the two was based on the same ties that had defined their relationship during the period of Nazi rule.[73]

Not only did the majority of Greeks fail to shed any tears for the victims of Serb aggression in Bosnia, many rallied in support of the indicted perpetrators of the crimes. Thus, within a few weeks after the announcement by the War Crimes Tribunal of the indictments of Radovan Karadžić and Ratko Mladić, the Greek-Serb Friendship Association was able to collect two million signatures for a declaration asking the tribunal to stop the prosecution of the two Serbs.[74] "We collected signatures everywhere," said treasurer Lykourgos Chazakos. "In the factories, in the offices, in the streets, in the neighbourhoods. The reaction of the people was overwhelming. We met with representatives of all political parties. They all showed tremendous understanding for our views. Especially encouraging were the people at the Ministry of Foreign Affairs."[75]

It may be of some interest to note that the Greek-Serb Friendship Association was subsidized by the Greek state. Thus, a list including the names of the nongovernmental organizations (NGOs) funded by the Greek Foreign Ministry that was published in January, 2001, revealed that during the previous year this organization received $200,000—a significant sum by Greek standards.[76]

With respect to the issue of human rights violations in Bosnia, both the New Democracy government and the PASOK government that succeeded it followed a two-faced policy. On one hand, Greece signed the various resolutions in the UN Security Council, NATO, and the EU condemning the human rights violations that were taking place. On the other hand, however, all Greek governments made certain that those decisions received little publicity in Greece. In most public statements and interviews, the Greek ministers at best attributed the blame for the mass atrocities in Bosnia equally to all the participants in the war or at worst avoided any mention of them—as if they had never taken place. "Greece," writes Alexis Heraklides, who at the time was employed at the Ministry of Foreign Affairs and is currently a senior lecturer at Panteion University in Athens, "showed indifference and failed to condemn the merciless bombing of civilian populations (Vukovar, Sarajevo) or the practice of ethnic cleansing simply because those acts happened to be committed by the Bosnian Serbs."[77] The Greek authorities stuck to the "everyone is equally to blame" line, even in the cases where the audience was Muslim and pro-Bosnian. The Greek ambassador to Tehran John Thomoglou, when asked in an interview with the Iranian daily *Resalat,* July 24, 1995, whether the Serb conduct was violating human rights, replied: "The war between the Serbs and the Muslims is a full-fledged war. Heinous acts have been committed by both sides. Sometimes one side commits a heinous act and sometimes it is the other side who commits a more heinous crime." In the few cases where the Greek government had no alternative but to condemn the Serbs for their atrocities, it resorted to an extreme legalese that was incomprehensible to most people.

Such was the case with Srbrenica. When Foreign Minister Karolos Papoulias learned that the city had fallen into the hands of the Bosnian Serbs, he condemned the act because it violated "Articles 819, 824, and 836 of the Security Council Resolutions."[78] Nevertheless, Papoulias voiced no concern about the atrocities that were almost certain to happen. Nor did any of the other Greek political parties, with the exception of the small left-wing party Sinaspismos, which condemned the event in the strongest of terms.

Belgrade understood perfectly well that the Greek signing of various EU, UN, and NATO communiqués condemning Serb human rights violations in reality meant nothing. Foreign Minister Jovanović revealed this during a visit to Greece in February, 1994. When asked by a journalist whether he was uncomfortable with the fact that Greece had signed some NATO and EU statements critical of Serbia's policies, he excused the Greeks by saying that they had been "forced" to sign those statements by their partners. "We understand," he said, "that although Greece signed those declarations, her heart lay elsewhere."[79]

The Greek government never protested Jovanović's assertion that it was not acting of its own free will. Nor did the Greek government take exception to Jovanović's statement that Greece's heart "lay elsewhere." The FRY foreign minister was right, though. The heart of Greece's political class did not lie in the killing fields of Srbrenica or Zvornik. Its heart indeed lay elsewhere. When Prime Minister Mitsotakis returned from a failed peace mission to Pale in April, 1993, he was reportedly ecstatic after having met Ratko Mladić and Radovan Karadžić all dressed up in battle gear. Mitsotakis told close relatives that they reminded him of the heroes of the Greek war of independence. His successor, Andreas Papandreou, who publicly called Radovan Karadžić "a peace fighter," was equally touched.[80]

Although both Mitsotakis and Papandreou paid scant attention to the issue of human rights violations in Bosnia, their reasons for doing so were different. As far as Mitsotakis was concerned, the few times I had the chance to raise the issue with him I got the impression that he was aware that atrocities were taking place. However, he seemed to consider this fact peripheral, something to be expected in a Balkan conflict. Papandreou's attitude was different. "Papandreou never raised the issue of human rights violations in our discussions," said Aris Mousionis, one of his advisers. "He believed that the reports about the atrocities the Serbs had committed were prefabricated and that in any case atrocities are parts of a war. We all believed at the time that the Serbs were the bearers of the international struggle against the New World Order and the plans of the imperialists. We believed that the fight of the Serbs didn't aim at the annihilation of the other ethnic groups but that it was directed against the forces of imperialism in the region."[81]

The charge of "duplicity" against the policies of the Greek governments vis-à-vis their partners in the European Community and NATO was a common one in the early 1990s. One of the main critics of Greece's policies was Daniel Cohn-Bendit, a member of the "Greens" in the European Parliament and one of the leading figures of the student uprising in Paris in May, 1968.

According to Cohn-Bendit, the Greek governments were playing a double game in the case of Serbia. To the West they stressed that Greece's traditional friendship with Serbia allowed it to act as a mediator. To the Serbs, on the other hand, they said that their good relations with the West allowed them to represent them. "I think," Cohn-Bendit concluded, "that what we are dealing with here is an extreme case of Levantine duplicity."[82] In the same vein, noted analyst Jacques Amalric also questioned the credibility of the Greek governments. Writing in the French daily *Liberation,* he posed the question as to whether "one would ever be able to forgive [French president] Valerie Giscard d'Estaing for letting Greece into the European Community?" Moreover, he continued: "We have known for quite sometime the sympathies of Greece for Mr. Milošević's Serbia and the violation by Greece of the embargo that has been imposed against the Belgrade regime even if the Western powers prefer to close their eyes. But today Greece by the very statements of some of its leaders dispels the myth concerning its purported non-involvement in the Balkan crisis and is thus destroying a priori its credibility as a mediator."[83]

Perhaps the duplicity did not remain only at the level of words. According to Aris Mousionis, Prime Minister Andreas Papandreou was leaking NATO military secrets regarding the air strikes the alliance had initiated on August 30, 1995, to the Bosnian Serb leadership and especially to General

Mladić. Mousionis, a doctor, in addition to being the founder and president of the Greek-Serb Friendship Association, advised Prime Minister Papandreou on the Bosnia war and was his personal intermediary with Radovan Karadžić and Slobodan Milošević. This fact has been widely reported in the Greek media.[84] In addition to having a Greek diplomatic pass issued to him on the personal orders of the prime minister, he also possessed a document carrying the signature of Greneral Mladić guaranteeing him safe conduct in the area controlled by the Bosnian Serbs.

"At the end of August, 1995, I was staying in a villa in Bosnia near the Serb border, which belonged to former prime minister Bjedić," Mousionis recalled during the interview. "I was guarded by about sixty soldiers—even my secretary and my cook were military people. During that period I was receiving messages from the Greek military headquarters in Athens which I was passing on to General Mladić. The information concerned the air strikes that NATO had initiated against the Bosnian Serbs. Only Andreas Papandreou knew the content of those messages—neither his minister of defense nor the chief of staff of the Greek armed forces [knew]. The sealed envelope containing the details of the planned NATO air strikes was directly delivered from the NATO's headquarters in Naples to Prime Minister Andreas Papandreou. He then gave the envelope with the plans to a person of his absolute confidence—whom only he and I knew—who took it to the military headquarters in Athens from where its contents were relayed to me. We used three codes because we had learned that the Americans had broken one. I received and immediately decoded the messages. I then gave them to Ratko Mladić's deputy commander, who delivered them personally to the General. Later, during the bombings, NATO intelligence found out that its plans were being leaked to the Bosnian Serbs and they stopped informing the Greeks, an event which led to strong protests by the latter."[85]

Let me stress here that I have not been able to obtain independent confirmation regarding Mousionis's claims. In May, 2001, former Greek defense minister Gerasimos Arsenis, who served in that capacity during NATO's air campaign in Bosnia, said that although he was aware of rumors that Greece was leaking NATO flight plans to General Mladić, an investigative committee he appointed to examine whether there was any truth to the allegations was unable to confirm them. When I asked him if it was possible Prime Minister Papandreou had personally transmitted the information without anybody knowing about it, he replied: "I doubt that Papandreou himself could have done such a thing. By that time his health was in a very poor state. He was extremely dependent on the people who were around him. I knew that he had independent channels of contact with General Mladić through a personal intermediary, a Greek doctor."

The Greek state's approach to the deliberations of the War Crimes Tribunal in The Hague can at best be characterized as dismissive. From the very beginning, the court was met with distrust. For example, PASOK government spokesman Evangelos Venizelos said: "The problem of Bosnia can only be solved by political means. It would be an unforgivable legalism to try to solve the problem with judicial means."[86] The Greek government's attitude toward the War Crimes Tribunal found its clearest expression in a statement by Theodore Pangalos, who at the time was the acting foreign minister of the PASOK government in power. After a meeting of European foreign ministers, he expressed strong objections to the deliberations of the tribunal because it was negatively predisposed toward the Serbs. He argued that because all sides had committed crimes, "it would be irrational to condemn Mr. Karadžić without looking for the corresponding leaders that have tolerated or promoted analogous acts. It is essential that we should stop demonizing only one side if we want peace and fairness."[87] This marked the first time the foreign minister of an EU or NATO member country made a statement challenging the impartiality of the UN War Crimes Tribunal. Moreover, the statement lent legitimacy to similar arguments used by Bosnian Serbs war criminals to justify their lack of cooperation with the tribunal.

Another fact revealing the Greek state's lack of interest in the subject of human rights violations and its unwillingness to assist the tribunal, was its failure to take action against the Greek paramilitaries who, some of their members admitted, were fighting alongside the Bosnian Serbs. During the war in Bosnia, Greek authorities ignored the open recruitment of people in Greece to fight against the legal government of Bosnia. They also did nothing to prevent the publicly organized collection of material help to support members of this fighting unit. In other words, the Greek government tolerated activities that arguably constituted acts of aggression against the sovereignty of a UN-recognized country and its government.

The "Greek Volunteer Guard," by the open and proud admission of its own members, took part in the events that led up to the murder of eight thousand innocent civilians in Srbrenica. Whenever the issue of the participation of Greek paramilitaries in the Srbrenica slaughter was raised, the Greek authorities kept feigning ignorance. When the Greek ambassador to Tehran John Thomoglou was asked about this incident by the Iranian daily *Resalat,* July 24, 1995, he replied, "Personally, I have not heard that Greek volunteers entered Srbrenica and hoisted the Greek flag."

In 1996 I asked a government spokesman whether the Greek government intended to investigate the activities of the individuals who had participated with the Bosnian Serb forces in the operations in Srbrenica and elsewhere. In the written reply I received, it was asserted that "Greece does not have any evidence concerning the involvement of Greek citizens in war-crimes in Bosnia-Herzegovina." I returned to this issue in January, 2000, when I sent a letter to Minister of Justice Evangelos Yannopoulos inquiring what steps he was thinking of taking in this matter. The reply I received from his spokesperson, a Mr. Georgoulis, the next day was: "The issue does not concern the minister."

In 1996 I asked Christos Rozakis, who later served as vice president of the European Court of Human Rights, to evaluate the Greek government's positions on the issues of human rights violations in the wars in the former Yugoslavia. Rozakis, who is also a close friend and senior adviser to Prime Minister Kostas Simitis replied: "At least the present [Simitis] government keeps a constructive silence. This is a big advance in relation to the previous ones that celebrated every time our Serb brethren committed a new horror."[88]

Christos Rozakis's story is particularly instructive. A professor of international law at the University of Athens, Rozakis had, since 1987, served as a member of the European Commission of Human Rights in the Council of Europe. After the fall, 1996, elections in Greece, Prime Minister Simitis appointed him deputy foreign minister. What was noteworthy about the appointment was that Rozakis was the most consistent and sophisticated critic of his country's foreign and human rights policies.[89] He had repeatedly argued that Greece's pro-Serbian attitude would result in its marginalization in the international community and he had also disagreed strongly with Greece's aggressive policies toward Macedonia. From the very moment Rozakis set foot in the Foreign Office he became the object of virulent attacks from the nationalist elements within his own party and the conservative opposition. The most obnoxious attack came from a deputy from the conservative New Democracy Party who asked the government to investigate Rozakis's Jewish origins because he thought they might "indicate suspect connections to enemy foreign powers." The reaction of the majority of the Greek political class was muted and the leader of the Greek Jewish community, Nasim Mais, expressed his "deep worry and disappointment." Rozakis stayed at the Foreign Office for five months. By early February, 1997, he felt he had had enough. He resigned and left Greece.[90]

CHAPTER 2

Plans for Macedonia

It would not be an overstatement to say that Greece's foreign policy during the first half of the last decade was dominated by a single issue: Macedonia.[1] On the surface, the argument concerned the name of the neighboring country. Greece refused to recognize its neighbor and prevented other EU countries from doing so because the neighbor had adopted Macedonia as its name. Greece argued that the adoption of this name was unacceptable for a number of reasons.

The first set of reasons related to the struggle over the control of symbols, traditions, historic lineage, and names—in sum, the paraphernalia that defines the contents of nationalist ideology. Greece claimed that the appropriation of the name Macedonia by its neighbor represented the "theft" or "usurpation" of Greek history and culture. From the Greek perspective, recognition of the Republic of Macedonia would therefore constitute an acceptance of the "theft" or "misappropriation of Greek cultural heritage" by a Slavic people. As Prime Minister Andreas Papandreou declared characteristically in a speech in Salonika in September, 1993, "our name is our life."[2]

The second set of reasons was less esoteric in nature. It concerned what Greece perceived as threats to its territorial integrity resulting from the adoption of the name by the neighboring country. Greece argued that the name Macedonia implied a claim to the neighboring Greek province of Macedonia and cited Tito's efforts to control it through the use of a partly Slavic communist guerrilla organization during the Greek civil war (1945–48).[3]

Evangelos Kofos, who orchestrated the Greek public relations effort, aptly summarized these two sets of reasons. The adoption of the name Macedonia, he argued, signaled "a double thrust and claim against Greece." One was territorial; the other concerned Greece's cultural and historical identity. By appropriating the name, it conveyed the impression that the republic has control over all things Macedonian.[4]

Those were the main arguments successive Greek governments and opinion makers presented to the international community and their NATO and EU allies and partners. If only the neighboring country would change its name, Greek officials said, nothing would stand in the way of a warm and friendly relationship between the two countries. Nevertheless, the truth was more complicated. There is a growing body of evidence indicating that at least some influential political forces in Greece during the early 1990s sought much more than a mere name change from their Macedonian neighbors. The real aim could, in some instances, be construed as being the destabilization of the young republic and its eventual demise. Some Greek politicians, using the name issue as a pretext, argued for a name change even though they knew fully well that no government in Skopje could plausibly comply. To do so would mean giving up the most important symbol of collective identity for the majority of the population. This was pointed out by Nicos Mouzelis, a professor at the London School of Economics, who wrote: "I wonder what sort of dialogue [the Greek side has in mind] when it refuses to negotiate the central issue [i.e. the name]."[5]

The suspicion that the name issue was only a pretext was widely shared outside Greece. According to Pavlos Sarlis, a Greek member of the European Parliament, "There are many who believe that this demand is aimed at precluding any possibility of Greek recognition of the Former Yugoslav Republic of Macedonia."[6]

Yet Greek officials went to great lengths, especially in statements directed to foreigners, to assure everybody that Greece objected only to its neighbor's name. "Greece," wrote Kofos, "does not dispute the existence of a nation, a language or a republic after 1944 but rather refuses the legitimacy of the appropriation of the Macedonian name for defining a Slavic people."[7] Nevertheless, this statement flew in the face of common sense. What the overwhelming majority of Greek society refused to accept was the existence of a "Macedonian" nation with its own history, language, and culture: "Greece refused to recognize either a Macedonian nation or a Macedonian state on the grounds that everything Macedonian—the name, the people, the history, the territory—were exclusively Greek." This refusal was based on the fundamental template that defines the nationalist ideology of modern Greece, namely the postulate of an unbroken historical continuity between ancient and modern Greece. This belief, Loring Danforth points out, combined with the belief that the ancient Macedonians were Greeks to produce the view that only Greeks could identify themselves as Macedonians.[8]

Thus, throughout the early and middle 1990s, in statement after statement by Greek politicians and in article after article in the Greek press, the Macedonian nation was referred to as "an artificial creation," "a counterfeit nation," and an "invention of Tito." At the same time, its inhabitants were referred to as "Skopjians," or "Macedonians" in quotation marks, or as "pseudo-Macedonians." Moreover, the Macedonian state was usually referred as a "formation" *(morfoma)* "statelet" *(kratidio),* or "hybrid" *(ivridio)*—terms indicating a serious deficiency in the state building capabilities of the young republic.[9] The same arguments were also used in relation to the Macedonian language. The Greek government and people consistently refused to accept the existence of a "Macedonian" language. The language would be described as a "local idiom " or "dialect"; " a spoken collection of words without syntax, without grammatical components, without spelling."[10] Greek linguist Giorgos Babiniotis edited a collection of essays that argue that the language of "Skopje" was "an artificial construction" created "from above" for political purposes.[11]

Perhaps the most comprehensive official denial of the existence of a Macedonian nation came from Foreign Minister Antonis Samaras on the occasion of Macedonian president Kiro Gligorov's visit to Ankara on September 10, 1991. Samaras chose that day to criticize the Turkish government for receiving "the ghost of the non-existent Macedonian nation."[12]

During the years 1991–93, the Greek authorities were not simply content with advancing their own viewpoints concerning Macedonia. They were also engaged in a systematic policy of harassment of Greek journalists and intellectuals who held dissenting opinions.[13]

Greece not only denied Macedonia's existence, it went so far as to advance the argument that the nonexistent Macedonian state was "nonviable," meaning that it was doomed to break up or become extinct. One of the most prominent Greek officials espousing this argument was Greek president Constantine Karamanlis. On February 26, 1992, he sent a three-page note to the Greek foreign minister claiming that both Bosnia and Macedonia were not viable states. According to Karamanlis, the dissolution of Yugoslavia had created a major crisis in Europe. The independence of only two of its parts, Slovenia and Croatia, had already resulted in much human sacrifice and material destruction. Moreover, preserving their independence was also very costly, requiring as it did the largest peacekeeping force in UN history. However, the problems caused by the relatively benign cases of Slovenia and Croatia paled in comparison to the much more serious consequences of hurriedly recognizing the independence of Bosnia and Macedonia without proper preconditions. He feared that "the ethnic composition and the geographical distribution of their population constitute an explosive mix" and that "their very viability as states is in doubt."[14]

An equally interesting, albeit little known, document in which a similar argument appeared was a memorandum on Yugoslav Macedonia submitted by Foreign Minister Samaras to his European colleagues on August 27, 1991. The context was a meeting of EU foreign ministers in The Hague. This document presented for the first time to the international community Greece's views concerning not only the fate of Macedonia but also that of Kosovo.[15]

According to Samaras, Kosovo and Macedonia could not survive as independent entities for economic, geopolitical, ethnological, and historical reasons. He then went on to predict that in both these regions a struggle would commence whose aim would be their annexation to their neighboring states. "A detached observer may well consider that an independent Macedonian state is hardly viable," he wrote. Economically, the landlocked state had no material basis for survival, and ethnologically more than a third of its population was composed of ethnic Albanians. Moreover, the ethnic origin of its Slav inhabitants was a cause for dispute. "They are currently named ethnic Macedonians," he noted, " but the Bulgarians and to lesser degree the Serbs claim them as their own."[16]

Those two documents, one from the head of state and the other from the foreign minister of an EU and NATO country, were quite revealing. The assertion that Macedonia was a "nonviable" state could easily be construed as providing carte blanche for outside intervention by third parties. If a state was "not viable," that is, if it was doomed to extinction, then it followed that outside intervention would not really amount to a destabilizing act but rather would merely speed up a process preordained by history and culture. Outside intervention in a nonviable state resembled more a case of assisted suicide than outright murder.

Let us forestall an objection here. It is indeed the case that arguments to the effect that ministates like Bosnia would not be able to survive in the long run were advanced by several analysts.[17] However, there are important differences. First, the expression of an analyst's personal opinion in a newspaper or academic journal does not carry the same weight as an official statement from the government of a country directly affected by events in the region. In the latter case, such a view can easily be interpreted as trying to legitimize outside intervention.Second, Greek reservations concerning the viability of Macedonia, Bosnia, and Kosovo focused particularly on their multiethnic character. What made those objections interesting was that they reflected the templates that define the ideology of modern Greece—namely ethnic nationalism. Greek objections to the viability of Bosnia and Kosovo derived not from an objective feasibility study but from a conception of the social order that rejects as "non-viable" the multiethnic or multicultural social model.[18]

Moreover, by placing the case of Macedonia alongside those of Bosnia and Kosovo, the statements by the Greek president and the foreign minister concerning the nonviability of the neighboring country could be construed not only as legitimizing the possibility of outside intervention, but also as prescribing from where the intervention should come. All three regions, according to Greek diplomacy, represent areas of the world whose inhabitants would never receive the blessings of statehood due to certain inherent "deficiencies" in their societal DNA. In two of the three cases mentioned, this deficiency was being corrected by the massive presence of Serb military and paramilitary forces. One might thus conclude that perhaps it was time for the same recipe to be applied in Macedonia, which up to that point had escaped the tragic fate of the other two countries.

Until 1996, when Kostas Simitis became prime minister, Greece followed policies that threatened Macedonia's stability. Those policies ranged from diplomatic attempts to block Macedonia's recognition by other EC countries and the imposition of economic blockades, to some more questionable and lesser-known policies involving Serbia's active cooperation. As far as the diplomatic efforts were concerned, from the beginning of 1991—when Macedonia became a sovereign state—the country's stability was being undermined by the Western powers' delay in extending diplomatic recognition and support following the collapse of Yugoslavia. "This delay," according to a report by the Center for Preventive Action, "stemmed from the efforts of Greece to block such recognition"[19]

The Arbitration Commission established as part of the EC conference on Yugoslavia decided in January, 1992, that Macedonia met all conditions for diplomatic recognition. But the EC failed to extend that recognition because its consensual decision-making process allowed Greece to veto the action. Delay of the collective recognition also delayed recognition by individual member states. In addition, Greece imposed a damaging unofficial embargo on trade in February, 1992, and an official one that summer over the strong objections of its EC partners.

To sidestep Greek objections to the use of the name "Macedonia," European members of the UN Security Council forged a compromise formulation in April, 1993, that allowed Macedonia to be admitted to the United Nations under the name "Former Yugoslav Republic of Macedonia" (FYROM). The same resolution called for Macedonia and Greece to begin negotiations to resolve outstanding issues.

Admission to the United Nations opened the door to wider diplomatic recognition. Albania recognized Macedonia the same month the compromise was announced, and Belgium extended diplomatic recognition in October, followed by Denmark, France, Germany, the Netherlands, and the United Kingdom in December. The United States extended recognition in February, 1994, although it withheld establishing full diplomatic relations in deference to the continuing Greek embargo.

"Recognition was widely seen in the West as a means to prevent the spread of fighting and as a necessary step towards stabilizing the internal politics of Macedonia itself."[20] Greece, however, did not share this view. The act of recognizing FYROM, viewed throughout Europe as strengthening the stabilization process in the Balkans, was seen in Greece as a hostile action directed against the Greeks. The 1993 election brought the socialist PASOK Party into power under aging leader Andreas Papandreou. The new government, committed to a hard line approach toward Macedonia, refused to participate in the face-to-face negotiations mediated by UN envoy Cyrus Vance, and closed the Greek-Macedonia border in February, 1994.

Negotiations continued in the form of proximity talks. That same month, the United States appointed a special representative to assist in the talks. After considerable pressure, especially from the Americans, Greece signed the agreement negotiated by UN envoy Cyrus Vance and his deputy ambassador, Herbert Okun, together with U.S. envoy Mathew Nimetz. The interim accord—signed at the United Nations on September 13, 1995—called for further negotiations to resolve remaining issues and formally ended the economic blockade. Nevertheless, the issue of recognition and of Macedonia's official name has yet to be resolved.

In the early 1990s, the Greek government seemed to be getting involved in another project of a more questionable nature. The project, which was to take place with the cooperation of Serbia, had as its aim the destabilization of Macedonia by a combination of economic and military means. From a geopolitical point of view this was without a doubt the most dangerous aspect of the Athens-Belgrade axis because it represented a serious threat to regional security. The reader should keep in mind that none of this was accomplished in a cultural vacuum. Throughout the years 1991–94, the rallying cry at mass rallies organized all around Greece was "Common Borders with Serbia" *("Koina Sinora me ti Servia"),* a slogan that implied a division of Macedonia between Serbia and Greece.[21] These ideas and thoughts did not remain only at the level of the printed word and popular imagination. There is now much hard evidence indicating that political leaders in Athens and Belgrade seriously entertained this adventurous scenario.

Throughout the years 1991–93, meetings between Prime Minister Constantine Mitsotakis and Minister of Foreign Affairs Antonis Samaras on one hand and Slobodan Milošević on the other invariably focused on the Macedonia "problem." These meetings, as well as the more general rapprochement between Greece and Serbia and the designs these two countries were thought to have on Macedonia, became a cause of concern for many in the West.[22]

No one, of course, was more worried than President Kiro Gligorov of the Republic of Macedonia. On January 16, 1992, during one of Milošević's frequent visits to Athens, Gligorov took the unusual step of issuing a statement in which he protested the fact that the Greek and Serbian leaders were discussing Macedonia's future without a Macedonian representative present.[23]

The worries of President Gligorov and the international community were not unfounded. Because what the leaders in Athens and Serbia were discussing in those meetings was truly disconcerting. We get a glimpse of the content of those discussions in an interesting little book written by Alexandros Tarkas, a senior policy adviser to the former Greek Minister of Foreign Affairs Antonis Samaras. In it, Tarkas reveals some of the behind-the-scenes plans being concocted by Greece and Serbia in the early 1990s. The book, which is based on confidential Greek Foreign Office documents and discussions with Greek and foreign diplomats, was endorsed by Samaras, who wrote the foreword. It should also be noted that none of the truly astonishing assertions made by the former Greek foreign minister's senior adviser have ever been challenged by either Greek or Serb officials.

The story, as described by Tarkas, started on August 8, 1991, when Slobodan Milošević held a long meeting with Lefteris Karagiannis, the Greek ambassador in Belgrade. At the start of the meeting, Milošević called Prime Minister Mitsotakis "my President friend" and at the same time expressed his "special appreciation" for Samaras and his "multidimensional active support" for Serbia in the EU.

After praising the two Greek politicians, Milošević told Karagiannis: "During the past few months I have discussed with your government the issue of Skopje. It is essential that our countries coordinate their policies."

The Greek ambassador agreed. "What more can we do?" he asked. "Many things," replied Milošević sharply. "A person in whom I have utmost confidence could visit Athens after the referendum in Macedonia on September 8, and we then can examine everything together." Karagiannis did not comment on the proposal but promised to convey it to Athens as soon as possible.[24]

The meeting that Milošević asked for did not take place in Athens. It took place a month later, on September 4, 1991, in Belgrade. Only two persons were present: Milošević and Samaras. The meeting, as described by Tarkas, is truly revealing of the way Slobodan Milošević's mind worked and of the strategy he followed in his attempt to create a Greater Serbia:

> After dinner, the Serb leader asked the Greek foreign minister to come upstairs to his office. Samaras stood up and followed Milošević, who climbed the marble staircase, went into his office, took out a file, consulted some codes, and asked the Greek foreign minister to follow him to a smaller and darker room. In the center of the room was a big table on which lay a map of the Balkans. "Look here," Milošević told Samaras, "in the center of FYROM (Macedonia) and especially in Tetovo and the surrounding areas live around 150,000 Serbs—not 40,000 as reported by the census."
>
> The Greek foreign minister immediately understood what his host had in mind and asked: "Do you mean to say that at one point or another they will face a problem and will have to move to a different location?" The Serb president revealed immediately what he meant: "They will move. Not only those but also thousands of other Serb refugees who are living in the north will move to the south toward Skopje, toward the Greek borders. Then Serbia and Greece will have common borders." The Greek foreign minister did not comment on the proposal. He merely said, "What you are telling me is very serious and I will convey your proposal to Mr. Mitsotakis. When Mr. (then–Prime Minister Constantine) Mitsotakis heard the proposal he just said, "I will think about it," but never returned to the issue.[25]

The proposal was vintage Milošević, involving, as it did, the use of local Serb populations as the key instrument for destabilizing neighboring countries.[26] But whereas in the case of Croatia and Bosnia his plans envisaged making use of existing local Serb minorities, in Macedonia, where there was no sizable local minority present, he was ready to create one by "exporting" Serb refugees from other parts of Serbia. This description, which has never been challenged by Serb authorities, is one of the most damning pieces of evidence concerning Milošević's strategy in Yugoslavia. It also proves that

8. *Greek prime minister Constantine Mitsotakis meets with Serbian president Slobodan Milošević in Athens in the fall of 1992. In the middle is Greek foreign minister Antonis Samaras. Photo courtesy* Prisma.

the last thing Slobodan Milošević had in mind when he was deciding his moves was the well-being of Serb minorities. For him, in an archetypal Balkan fashion, the Serb minorities were useful only to the extent that they promoted his expansionist dreams.

The plan he outlined to Samaras involved two-steps: inflating beyond recognition the number of ethnic Serbs residing in the area and, at the same time, instigating a massive influx of civilians to Macedonia from Serbia. The final step would involve, as happened elsewhere, sending the Yugoslav army to "protect" the Serb minority. This would result in the collapse of Macedonia as an independent entity and its absorption into Serbia.

What is most interesting about the meeting was the total lack of any negative reaction or comment by Greece's minister of foreign affairs to a proposal that involved a serious violation of international legality. It is perhaps worth noting that Milošević had by then begun calling Macedonia "Skopje" to please the Greeks.[27]

Milošević's proposal did not come out of the blue. When Macedonia followed Slovenia and Croatia in declaring its independence from the former Yugoslavia in 1992, the Serb president was outraged and accused Macedonia of "stabbing him in the back." However, since he was already committed to wars in Croatia and Bosnia-Herzegovina, there was little he could do militarily to prevent Macedonia's departure. He thus decided to turn to Greece for military assistance to help him in his plans to bring Macedonia to heel. For his part, he would seek to undermine the young republic by encouraging Macedonian Serb extremists. Inspired by his promptings, Macedonia's Democratic Serbian Party, formed after the republic declared its independence, set about trying to establish a separate "Karadag Republic" in the northern parts of the country where most Serbs live: Skopska Crna Gora (Skopje Black Mountain) and Kumanovska Dolina (Kumanovo Valley). Although party members boasted of meeting with Bosnian Serb military leader Ratko Mladić in Pale and of attending military training courses, they were unable to muster enough support to mount an uprising.

Milosević's proposal did not totally surprise his Greek friends. In fact, similar ideas were being entertained at the Greek Foreign Ministry. The idea of Macedonia's eventual annexation by Serbia was by no means alien to the Greek government. Indeed, it was already being openly proclaimed in official and semiofficial Greek documents. The first such document was the Memorandum on Yugoslav Macedonia, mentioned earlier in this chapter. In it, the Greek government predicted that Macedonia would declare its independence in the event Yugoslavia dissolved. According to the memorandum, such an initiative was bound to have cataclysmic consequences for the entire Balkan region. Bulgaria had already declared that it would recognize an independent Macedonian state, apparently expecting that in the context of such a state its inhabitants—currently called "Macedonians"—would rediscover their "Bulgarian roots." Any Bulgarian initiative in that direction, the memorandum predicted, would face stiff opposition not only from die-hard Slav-Macedonian nationalists but also from Serbs. The latter would undoubtedly consider such developments as threatening their own vital interests. "For historical reasons, the Serbs may claim that what constitutes the Republic of Macedonia was traditionally a Serbian land. But more important, they may be induced to intervene for fear that an independent Republic of Macedonia aligned with Bulgaria might cut off their commercial access to the Aegean ports of Greece."[28]

While this document merely shows that the Greek government was aware of Serb plans or threats to destabilize Macedonia, another semiofficial publication indicates that Greece was not averse to the idea of a Serbian take-over of Macedonia. The latter document is an interesting propaganda book-let titled "The Macedonian Affair: A Historical Review of the Attempts to Create a Counterfeit Nation," which the Greek Foreign Ministry distrib-uted to Greek and foreign journalists.

After repeating the standard mantra that Macedonia did not fulfill the preconditions of being a "viable state" because of its suspect ethnological composition, this semiofficial publication argues that the creation of the state by Tito had as its only purpose the harming of Serbian interests: "It is a historically indubitable fact that the so-called Republic of Macedonia is identified with the creation, by Tito, of the Federal Republic of Yugoslavia, whose main objective was to restrict and weaken Serbia."[29]

In essence, the Greek Foreign Office pamphlet simply repeated and adopted as its own the Serb view on the matter.[30] Those views, in effect, legitimized the claims Serbia had on the young republic. When it is argued, as was the case here, that a country is not "viable" because it was created as part of an effort to "restrict and weaken Serbia," then it follows that the annexation of that country by Serbia would at the very least not run counter to the demands of historical justice.

It is true that Mitsotakis did not endorse Milošević's plan as presented to him by Samaras. On the other hand, neither did he object to his Foreign Ministry's adoption in early 1992 of a plan that would involve Greece and Serbia in a common effort to destabilize Macedonia. "The Greek side, and especially the Greek Foreign Ministry, made the utmost use of Milošević's offer when in February and March of 1992 it applied the so-called Samaras Pincer on Skopje."[31]

This plan consisted of two strategic moves. The first consisted of apply-ing economic pressure to Macedonia so as to provoke riots and instability in the country. This task would be undertaken by Greece and would primarily involve the imposition of an economic blockade against the young republic. The second involved applying military pressure, a task to be undertaken by the Yugoslav army's 3d Division, which was stationed in Macedonia.

On one hand, the plan relied on the expected effects of the economic pressure Greece could exert by disrupting the flow of petrol to Macedonia, and on the other hand "on the presence of the Third Division of the Yugoslav Army, which had not as yet departed from Skopje. Its mere presence made Gligorov a prisoner of Milošević—in full collaboration with Athens."[32] In February, 1992, the Greek Foreign Ministry decided to set in motion the economic arm of the "Samaras Pincer" by imposing an unofficial embargo

on the movement of goods to Macedonia. This was not the official embargo
that the Greek Government imposed against Macedonia later that summer.
This was an unofficial embargo that received little publicity abroad. Indeed,
as official documents reveal, the Greek government's intention was to hide
the fact that it was applying economic sanctions against Macedonia so as
not to incur the wrath of the European Community.

The Ministry of Foreign Affairs instructed customs officials to tighten
the border controls. Documents and certificates that up to that time had
been considered mere formalities suddenly became of paramount importance. One such case involved the stamp Macedonian authorities put on the
various documents accompanying goods. Greek customs officials abruptly
started refusing to accept documents bearing the stamp with the name "Republic of Macedonia." The effects "on Skopje were dramatic since Salonika
was its main supplier while at the same time the Salonika harbor served as
the main transit center for Skopje's trade with third countries. . . . Samaras's
discreet economic pressure brought quick results: The shortage of petrol
and raw materials dislocated all sectors of Skopje's economy in a very short
period."[33]

The Greek government tried to hide the imposition of an economic
embargo on Macedonia from its European partners. This was made clear in
a revealing reply the foreign minister sent to the prefect of Salonika Evgenios
Chaitidis. When the prefect complained that certain Greek petroleum companies were trying to get around the embargo by various means, the foreign
minister replied on March 3, 1992: "I am hereby giving you in writing the
clear instruction to proceed using all means at your disposal to undertake
actions that will increase the economic pressure on Skopje. In view of the
initiatives the European Community has undertaken, our Ministry does
not think it would be advisable to officially seal the borders for the time
being."[34]

The aim of the embargo was to create social unrest and destablize the
Macedonian government. This was revealed in a letter Foreign Minister
Samaras sent to Prime Minister Mitsotakis on March 17, 1992: "It is obvious
that such developments will strengthen the reactions of the people of Skopje
to their government and they will multiply the phenomena of mass demonstrations that are being organized across the state against the intransigent
position of their government."[35]

At the same time, the Greek government, acting in the context of the
"Samaras Pincer," was encouraging Milošević to apply military pressure to
Macedonia with the army's 3d Division stationed in Skopje. According to

the senior adviser to the Greek foreign minister, "Our Ministry of Foreign Affairs was very happy with the political and psychological blackmail Belgrade exerted on Skopje."[36] A state of affairs existed where, as the author pointed out, any order emanating from even the lowest-ranking Serb army officer was sufficient to neutralize any political decision taken by the government of Macedonia. This constantly undermined the authority of President Gligorov.

Greece's cooperation with Serbia was not only restricted to the "Samaras Pincer" plan. Soon after the Samaras-Milošević meeting, the Greek government announced the existence of a repressed Greek ethnic minority in Macedonia. A classified Greek military intelligence report dated May 10, 1991, was leaked to the press. The report claimed that 239,360 Greeks lived in Macedonia—people of "pure" Greek national consciousness who saw themselves "descending from the Greek race" and who did not enjoy any minority rights. The report further suggested that a "formal statement by the Greek government asking for the protection of this Greek minority would serve Greek national interests in the region."[37] The Greek government officially adopted the policy recommended in the report, and on November 2, 1991, Deputy Foreign Minister Virginia Tsouderou declared that there were "150,000 Vlachs of pure Greek national consciousness" living in Macedonia. By a strange coincidence, the announcement came the same day Serbian vice president Budimir Kosutić stated that there were three hundred thousand Serbs in Macedonia.[38]

In a similar vein, Irineos Bulović, the bishop of Novi Sad, told a Greek television interviewer that Macedonia was created to stand between and separate old friends and allies: "This country contains both Greek and Serbs, therefore Greece must claim one part of Macedonia and Serbia the other."[39] The two countries would thus realize their old dream of acquiring common borders.

More statements of a similar nature soon followed. According to Željko Ražnatovic, the leader of Serb paramilitary forces better known as "Arkan": "This ghost-state was created by the communist Tito in order to separate Greece from Serbia." The Serb warlord said two hundred thousand Serbs lived in Macedonia, a fact that gave Serbia every right to take the part that belonged to it and was part of historic Serbia. "Of course," he continued, "you also have the right to take what remains. It is your natural northern border. Whatever will remain from this state will belong to you."[40]

Not everybody in Greece was equally euphoric about the sudden discovery of fellow ethnics in Macedonia. One of the dissenters, left-wing analyst

9. *Serbia's President Slobodan Milošević with PASOK leader Andreas Papandreou in Athens in the spring of 1991. In the middle is Milošević's son Marko. Photo courtesy Gregoris Rentzis.*

Aggelos Elefantis, wrote: "Just as nationalism constructs history on its own terms, it also constructs enslaved fellow ethnics in enemy territory."[41]

It was obvious that claims concerning the purported existence of "oppressed" Greek and Serb minorities in Macedonia were increasing the tension in the region. The deployment of U.S. troops in Macedonia as part of a UN peacekeeping force in July, 1993, helped defuse the tension. According to Macedonia's deputy minister of foreign affairs, the move prevented the realization of the plans certain neighboring countries had for Macedonia.[42] Regardless of the accuracy of this assessment, the fact remains that the deployment of U.S. forces took place *after* the Bush administration had been advised by the Central Intelligence Agency that a flare-up was imminent and that it would definitely involve Greece and Turkey.[43]

The close cooperation between the Greek government and the Belgrade regime continued even after the change of government in Greece. Thus, on February 16, 1995, Prime Minister Andreas Papandreou announced his government's decision to interrupt the transportation of merchandise to and from Skopje through the port of Thessaloniki. The decision to impose the embargo was apparently intended to protest a string of announcements by

Greece's allies recognizing Macedonia. The latest of these was made by the United States that same month. What was most noteworthy, however—and indicative of the fact that the Greek-Serbian "deep" cooperation continued to flourish—was the fact reported in the Greek media that the prime minister had informed President Milošević of the impending embargo one week before the measure was implemented. The information was conveyed to the Serb president by Foreign Minister Karolos Papoulias, one of the few people Papandreou really trusted, who traveled to Belgrade explicitly for that purpose.[44]

However, Macedonian authorities never took the threat of outright Greek military intervention seriously. According to Kiro Gligorov, the soft-spoken former president of Macedonia, the real danger lay elsewhere. "We were always afraid of Milošević's Serbia," he told me. "We never considered Greece a real threat because we knew that she was constrained in her actions by her membership in the European Union and above all in NATO."[45]

CHAPTER 3

The Blame Game

At half past noon on Saturday, February 5, 1994, a large mortar round exploded in the marketplace of Sarajevo, the capital of Bosnia. The result: sixty-nine dead and two hundred wounded. Men, women, and children. This criminal act provoked outrage in the international community against the Serbs, who were immediately blamed for the incident. After all, it was the Bosnian Serbs who possessed large-caliber guns and were shelling the city on a daily basis.

The Serbs denied responsibility for the carnage, which they attributed to Muslim terrorists. The aim, they argued, was to force the international community to intervene on behalf of the Muslims. After analyzing the shell burst, UN ordnance experts still were unable to determine from where it was fired.

A week later, on February 18, a second "shell" landed. This time, happily enough, it was only a media event. During the course of a television interview, French journalist Bernard Volker revealed that a UN report indicated the mortar round was fired from the Muslim sector of the city. The French journalist's revelations resulted in a storm of protest. Many challenged Volker's story. Some even accused him of being part of the "disinformation machine" that was set in motion immediately after the incident.[1] Volker, meanwhile, refused to present any evidence or to reveal his sources, a fact that made his story even more suspect.

Finally, on Friday, March 18, the French journalist decided to show his cards. And then a third "shell" exploded. Volker chose that occasion to reveal that the Greek Foreign Office was his source of information. According to Volker, his story was based on a telegram that had come into his possession. The telegram, signed by the official EU mediator, Lord David Owen, referred to a story issued by the Serbian news agency Tanjug announcing that UN sources had stated that the mortar shell was fired from the Muslim sector of Sarajevo. Owen, however, did not adopt the Tanjug version of events; he merely quoted from it. Then, following normal procedures, he sent his telegram to the Foreign Office of the country that occupied the presidency of the EU, in this case Greece, which was responsible for its further distribution to the member states.

The process functioned properly except for one thing: In the course of transmission, the quotation marks on the Tanjug material disappeared. The result was that somebody reading the telegram would think that its sender was endorsing the Tanjug version of events.

"I had no reason," said Volker, "to believe that a confidential official report could be altered due to either a printing error or a conscious effort to distort it."[2] The Greek Ministry of Foreign Affairs, headed at the time by PASOK minister Karolos Papoulias, did not issue a statement. In private, its officials dismissed the French journalist's story as "ridiculous." The story thus was left to rest since nobody in his right mind would ever believe that the foreign ministry of an EU and NATO country would dare to distort a document in order to whitewash the Serbs.

That was the way matters stood until November, 1995, when David Owen's memoir, *Balkan Odyssey*, appeared. Owen's account seemed to confirm Volker's story. Owen said that he knew at the time that Tanjug was about to issue a story saying the Serbs expected UN ballistics experts to confirm the content of leaked UN documents stating that the shell that caused the tragedy in Sarajevo's marketplace was fired from some one to one and one-half kilometers inside Muslim-controlled territory. Owen claimed that he sent the Tanjug dispatch, in quotes, in a telegram dated February 12. "Unfortunately," he added, "the Greek presidency transmitted the COREU [telegram] without the quotes so that at a later stage, when we had our first leak of my COREU telegrams, it was construed that the passage in my telegram, without quotes, was my opinion rather than Tanjug's."[3]

All this was, of course, highly embarrassing to the Greek government. The change in the original telegram could have been due to a technical error in transmission. However, if that was the case, why did the Greek government not make the story public at the very start, thereby putting a stop to all the speculation concerning the possible origin of the mortar round? What was the point in letting the speculation and confusion continue? It must also be noted that Foreign Minister Papoulias was a staunch supporter of Slobodan Milošević, as well as a vocal critic of NATO's presence in the region. Papoulias's anti-NATO pronouncements and statements became more frequent and strident after he left the Foreign Office. During an interview aired on a Greek radio station in March, 2001, he claimed that the sole purpose of NATO's military presence in the region is to "wipe Serbia off the map, politically and militarily"—an event that would deprive Russia of its sole European ally.[4]

The story does not end there. It took an even more curious turn the following year. Owen, in response to my request for clarification of some points related to the incident, withdrew the embarrassing revelations he had made in his book about the way the Greek Foreign Office handled the affair and shifted the blame to his secretary.

"I have never had any doubts," he wrote in a letter dated June 6, 1996, "that this was simply a mistake in transmission from my office in Geneva to the Greek Foreign Ministry and that there was nothing whatever sinister in the event."

Why did he change his mind? One must consider some facts.

First, who benefited from the confusion created in the West by the Greek presidency's COREU? The Serbs, primarily, but also other parties in the West who, for various reasons, were opposed to NATO intervention at the time. By sowing confusion concerning the origins of the Sarajevo tragedy, the telegram and the resulting story had the effect of preventing public outrage reaching levels that would force the leaders of NATO countries to undertake an immediate military response against the Serbs. In other words, the telegram and the confusion created by Volker's revelations probably contributed to the postponement of military action by NATO forces.

One must also bear in mind that the two main actors in this drama, the Greek government and Lord Owen, were of the same mind as far as the issue of military action against the Serbs was concerned. They both opposed it, although for perhaps different reasons. As far as Greece was concerned, this was a basic pillar of its foreign policy. The "Orthodox brethren" should never be punished for their crimes, come what may. Greece was the only one among the fifteen members of the alliance that dissented from the decision made by the NATO Alliance Council on February 9, 1994. After ten hours of discussion, the council reached a decision that gave the Serbs ten days to withdraw or regroup and place under UN Protection Force (UNPROFOR) control all their heavy weapons—tanks, artillery pieces, missiles, multiple rocket launchers, and so forth. It also asked the Bosnian government to put its heavy weapons under UNPROFOR control. The decision defined the exclusion zone as twenty kilometers from the center of Sarajevo, excluding an area within two kilometers of Pale, the Bosnian Serb capital.

Greece objected to this decision on the ground that it presented the Serbs with an ultimatum: "The Greek Government believes that this aim [i.e., the demilitarization of Sarajevo] by violent means is not only meaningless but at the same time runs the danger of leading to negative results that will cancel out the whole effort of achieving an agreement by all interested parties in this matter."[5] However, Greece's efforts to prevent NATO from bombing the Serbs may not have been restricted only to the expression of dissent with the decision of the Alliance Council. According to sources in Skopje, the Greek government's decision to impose the second embargo on Macedonia on February 14, 1994, was related to NATO's ultimatum to bomb the Serbs.

Thus, the Social Democratic Union, which constituted President Gligorov's political power base, declared that it "is noteworthy that the decision by the Greek government [to impose the embargo] comes at a time when it is trying to prevent NATO from enforcing its ultimatum." Moreover, according to reports published in the weekly Macedonian paper *Puls,* the Greek embargo on Macedonia had little or no relation to the standing disagreement between the two countries concerning Macedonia's name, but instead was related to events in Bosnia. "Mr. Papandreou," wrote the paper, "expressed by this act his displeasure about the fact that his country's allies do not take into consideration the Greek viewpoint and the Greek initiatives when forming their policies in relation to the crisis in Bosnia." The paper also argued that with the imposition of the embargo, "Andreas Papandreou helps his friend Milošević to relieve himself from the immense pressures he is facing." Finally, the paper insisted that the Greek measures were taken "in cooperation with Belgrade."[6]

There is, of course, no way of knowing whether those allegations were true. Nevertheless, it is a fact that the Greek media extensively reported that Papandreou informed Milošević of the impending act a week before Greece imposed the embargo.[7] He was the only foreign political leader the Greek government informed of an act that would once again throw the European Community and NATO into turmoil and cause tremendous soul searching among Greece's allies and friends.

Another piece of information that lends credibility to the *Puls* story regards the immediate endorsement of the Greek move against Macedonia by the Bosnian Serb leadership. Radovan Karadžić appeared on the popular Greek television talk show *Profile* the same day the Greeks imposed the embargo and expressed his strong and unconditional support for it.

On the other hand, Lord Owen's reasons for opposing military action against the Serbs were more complex. They may have reflected to a certain extent his personal belief that the Serbs had not fired the mortar round. Noel Malcolm, who reviewed *Balkan Odyssey* in the *Sunday Telegraph,* observed: "When discussing the February 1994 marketplace massacre in Sarajevo, Lord Owen goes on at length about a UN investigation which concluded that the mortar shell had been fired from a Bosnian government position. He dramatically confirms that General Rose put pressure on Bosnian ministers by threatening to reveal his findings unless they did as they were told. What Lord Owen did not tell us is that a second, more thorough, investigation found that the first had made mistakes in the calculations and concluded that the shell could also have come from the Serb side."[8]

In trying to untangle the mystery of the COREU telegram concerning the Sarajevo marketplace mortar blast, one must also bear in mind the smooth working relationship that had developed between Lord Owen and successive Greek governments. What they shared, among other things, was a worldview that led to a consistent downplaying of Serb atrocities.

This can be seen in a revealing conversation Lord Owen had with Foreign Minister Michalis Papakonstantinou. In this conversation, which took place during the dinner following the EU foreign ministers' conference in London in September, 1992, Lord Owen appeared to be expressing the view that the Muslims were equally—if not in fact more so—to blame for the crimes committed in Bosnia.

According to Foreign Minister Papakonstantinou:

My last conversation before going to sleep was with Lord Owen. I started talking to him as soon as he finished talking to my wife. He seemed to be a person of rare abilities and decisiveness. He was asking my opinion about the situation in the Balkans. I was the only who argued that the Serbs alone could not be guilty. The Muslims argued that the Serbs raped twenty thousand women. "What the hell," I asked him, "are the Serbs making war or love?" It was discovered that only two or three hundred Muslim women had been raped and that they had been taken to Germany to give birth. The other side was obviously committing the same crimes. Guilt in a war cannot be one sided. Owen agreed with me. By then he very strongly held the opinion that the Muslims were equally to blame. In some instances they were more to blame than the Serbs.[9]

The smooth relationship that had developed between the Greek Foreign Ministry and Lord Owen led the EU mediator to occasionally accept as true Greek claims that were eventually proven to be false. A case in point concerned his uncritical acceptance of the Greek claim that the Macedonian government had put "on their stamps a Greek castle on the sea at Thessalonica which shows a more than theoretical claim on Greek territory."[10] A few days later it was revealed that the picture was simply an advertising gimmick used by a small Macedonian tobacco company.

Finally, it is worth noting that Lord Owen's understanding of the Greek views both in relation to FYROM as well as to the mayhem in the former Yugoslavia may have been related to more than the fact that they both opposed military action against the Serbs. The overlap in their views reflected the British Foreign Office's emphasis on the primacy of national interest over closer European integration. Throughout the war in Bosnia, the British Foreign Office found itself in the intriguing position of occasionally disagreeing with the substance of the Greek views concerning the Balkans crisis while at the same time having to support Greece's right to dissent from the views of the rest of the European Community.[11]

"My job," wrote Lord Owen, "was to do everything possible to keep the Twelve together and I had no interest or wish to isolate the Greeks. I have an abiding political belief that the European Community cannot survive if it stifles the legitimate upholding of national interests and that its future design should not attempt to prevent the expression of a genuine national interest."[12]

May it then be that Lord Owens's desire to "protect " the Greeks—thereby protecting British foreign policy—was responsible for his about-face concerning the mistake in the telegram? Is it possible that, as soon as he realized the issue was becoming the focus of a media investigation, he decided to shift the blame to his secretary so as not to "isolate" the Greeks? At this point there is no way of knowing where the truth lies.

The Saloon Leonard lies a hundred meters from the center of Foča/Srbinje, a small town near Radovan Karadžić's headquarters in Pale. The cafe and gambling lounge was a popular hangout for local Mafiosi and indicted Bosnian Serb war criminals. They would sit there sipping their slivovitz, unperturbed by either the French troops—part of the stabilization forces (SFOR) serving in Bosnia under NATO's mandate—occasionally patrolling the streets or the United Nations International Police Task Force (IPTF) station just five minutes away.

Located high up in the mountains, Foča was the scene of one of the worst cases of ethnic cleansing. Prior to the war, the majority of its forty thousand inhabitants were Bosnian Muslims. The twenty-five-thousand-strong Muslim population was forcefully evicted in 1992, and many of their homes and buildings—including cultural masterpieces like the sixteenth century Aladža mosque—were destroyed. Today, the entire population of the town—recently renamed Srbinje ("Town of the Serbs")—consists of Bosnian Serbs.

The indicted war criminals who roamed the streets in this town and others throughout the Bosnian Serb republic acted as if they owned the place, which they did. The fact that the indicted were in control became obvious during the first briefing Organization for Security and Cooperation in Europe (OSCE) officials gave to a team of international observers who had come for the September, 1997, municipal elections. We were told not to go out after 8 P.M. and to keep out of the way of Foča's indicted war criminals—including Dragan Gigović, Janko Janjić and Bojko Jancović. I later learned that this was easier said than done.

A few days after our arrival, I was walking with my interpreter—a young Serb refugee from Sarajevo—in the former Muslim part of the city taking pictures. An individual suddenly appeared out of a little cafe where he had obviously been drinking and ordered me to stop taking pictures. At the same time, he demanded in a threatening manner to see my identity document. All this happened in the presence of two local Bosnian Serb policemen, who nodded approvingly. Assuming by his demeanor that he was a local official, I obeyed. What was striking about him was that both his hands were covered by snake tattoos.

When he saw my Greek passport his mood changed completely. A smile lit up his face and he said, "Greeks and Serbs are brothers!" He then embraced me and began pulling me toward the cafe where he had been sitting to offer me a drink. "Together we will fuck the Muslims!" he said gleefully.

Greek journalists always had privileged access to Serb war criminals. While in Zvornik on a journalistic mission, Christina Korai from *Eleftherotypia* came across Serb warlord Arkan and Russian nationalist leader Vladimir Zhirinovsky. They were dining together in the Hotel Yugoslavia surrounded by bodyguards.

"Since I knew that it was very hard to get near to Arkan," she wrote in her dispatch, "I went to one of his people and said, 'I am a Greek journalist and I want to talk to Arkan.' I knew how much Arkan liked Greek journalists. His bodyguard went and told him. Arkan looked at me and answered that the only reason he was going to talk to me was because I was Greek."[13]

In any event, I managed to shake off my new acquaintance and walked away. However, I promised him that the next time we met I would join him in celebrating the Greek-Serb alliance over some glasses of *raki*. I later found my newfound friend was the infamous Janko Janjić, who had been nicknamed "the Snake" because of the serpent tattoos that covered his body. He was wanted by The Hague International War Crimes Tribunal to answer charges of engaging in ethnic cleansing and rape against the Muslims in Foča. The indictment accuses Janjić of committing crimes in 1992 when he was a military police subcommander and paramilitary leader there.

I returned with an interpreter two days later and again encountered the Snake on the street outside the Saloon Leonard. He was initially happy to see me and repeated his invitation to join him for a drink. This time he tried to entice me with an offer to tell me stories about what he had done to the Muslims. "You write those stories in your newspaper?" he inquired. "In Greece they like those stories, yes?"

"What sort of stories?" I asked through my interpreter.

"Fuck Muslims!" he said, jerking his body backward and forward in case I misinterpreted the semantics. "Partizan Stadium—fuck, fuck, fuck!"

The Partizan Sports Hall, an architectural monstrosity in the middle of Foča, was the place where the Bosnian Serbs had kept most of the Muslim women and children in 1992. Every night it was filled with the cries of women who were being raped, sometimes in front of their small children.

He no doubt had some interesting stories to tell. Like the following one recorded by Amnesty International:

> During the 10 days that one 12-year-old girl was detained at the Partizan Sports Hall in August 1992, she said that she was taken out of the center 10 times to be raped; her mother was taken twice."

Or this one:

> Fikreta's four-year-old daughter was also taken with her. She was able to watch through an open door as her mother was stripped, searched for valuables, and a pistol was put to her head. She reported that she was then raped by four men. "They told me they would like us to give birth to Cetnic children. They told me 'we will do everything so that you never think of returning.'"[14]

Those were really great stories. It was doubtful, however, that my newspaper—or any other Greek newspaper for that matter—would be very eager to run them. The newspaper and the journalists filing the stories could expect an avalanche of phone calls denouncing them as "Muslim agents" or—even worse—"NATO agents" and threatening their physical safety. The cultural syntax of Greek ethnic nationalism was incapable of generating meaningful sentences about atrocities committed by the "Orthodox brethren." Which perhaps is as it should be. As Maria Todorova assures us, being critical of the Serb practice of systematic rape is tantamount to committing the cardinal crime of "balkanism."[15] The essence of this methodological crime, if I understand her correctly, consists in adopting a critical stance toward the pain and suffering the nations of the region have been inflicting upon one another during the last century.

Meanwhile, the Snake had changed his tune. Now he wanted money. "Hundred dollars!" he said. I refused as politely as I could. "Fifty!" he said, adding, "You don't like my stories?"

I could see that his mood was turning nasty. He probably suspected that there was something wrong with me since I had failed to show the enthusiasm he expected from an Orthodox "brother." Suddenly he started screaming that he was going to slit our throats. At the same time, some of his friends, drawn by his shouting, started coming out of the saloon.

"Run!" my Serb interpreter cried. We did a U-turn and headed at full speed for the IPTF station a block away. We immediately reported the incident to the OSCE field officer in Foča and an emergency meeting that included the commanding officer of the French SFOR troops and the IPTF was held. The SFOR is empowered by the Dayton accords to arrest indicted war criminals.

The fact that the Snake had threatened the life of an international observer and a Serb citizen (my interpreter) provided an additional basis for action. After much deliberation the authorities reached a momentous decision: they would ask the Serb police to please tell the Snake not to harass foreigners. Talking to the French SFOR officials made me feel like home. It was as if I were talking to officials at the Ministry of Foreign Affairs in Athens.

The decision was reached despite my protests that turning the case over to the local police—all of whom were Karadžić loyalists—endangered not only my safety but also that of my interpreter, who had testified against Janjić during the informal hearing. I did not suffer the consequences of this decision as I was soon evacuated, nor did I ever learn what happened to my young Serb friend after our departure. The incident, which later appeared in an Amnesty International report, was only the latest—and by no means most serious—in a whole series of aggressive acts that went unanswered in Foča during that year.[16]

In December, two cars belonging to the OSCE were blown up. In July, a hand grenade blew up a car belonging to the European Community Monitoring Mission. In August, an Italian member of an NGO was dragged out of his car in the middle of the city by a group that included some of the indicted war criminals and beaten up in full view of IPTF officers who did nothing. Later that month, an IPTF policeman was stopped by the same group and had a hand grenade placed under his armpit "for fun." According to witnesses, the same group of indicted war criminals was involved in all these incidents. Nor was any action ever taken in any of these cases—no doubt for the same reason I was told they would not arrest the Snake: They did not want to disturb the good relations they had with the local community.[17]

The attitude in Greece toward the issue of mass rapes in Bosnia was in many ways the same as that toward of the rest of the crimes committed by the Serbs. Indifference. However, in the case of the rapes, there was another factor at play: the attitude that rape is a part of war, that it is a sort of psychological relief mechanism for stressed-out warriors, and that, in the final analysis, "everybody was doing it." This attitude was not restricted to Greece. According to Stjepan Meštrović, the West had erected "mental mechanisms against the suggestion that rape can be and is used as a weapon of war and genocide."[18] It was quite some time before the West realized that Serb acts of rape were not a form of Reichian orgone therapy, but rather another tactic used in carrying out their strategy of ethnic cleansing.

The practice of ethnic cleansing, observes Susan Woodward, should not be seen as an expression of ethnic hatred or other emotional states but as a political strategy aimed at obtaining land.[19] Subjecting Muslim women and young girls to the degradation of rape was the best way to insure that they would never return to their villages. This also explains why so many elderly Muslim matrons were among the rape victims. This act makes sense as soon as one realizes that the Serbs committed rape not because they needed sex but because they wanted ethnically purified territories.

Eventually the West realized the purpose of the mass rapes. But not Greece. Even as late as the year 2001, while the trial of the perpetrators of the Foča rapes was being conducted by the International War Crimes Tribunal, prominent members of the Greek legal establishment were accusing Western legal experts of showing bias by dealing only with cases involving Muslim women. This charge was leveled by none other than Aliki Yotopoulou-Marangopoulou, president of Greece's National Human Rights Commission. In 1993 she was the Greek government's representative to the EU commission set up to investigate the alleged rape of Muslim women in the former Yugoslavia. The commission, which was formed in December, 1992, was presided over by Ann Warburton, Great Britain's EU ambassador, and included women representing each of the EU's twelve member states. In January, 2001, as the tribunal's Foća rape proceedings were nearing their end, Yotopoulou-Marangopoulou accused the Warburton Commission of being one-sided. She claimed it had turned down her request to investigate possible instances of rape involving women of other ethnic groups. She said the only reason she remained with the commission was that she wanted "to see to what lengths those plotting the situation would go." She explained that the only reason "the Commission findings reached the UN" in the first place was as "a result of those plots, fabricated by centers outside Europe."[20]

CHAPTER 4

The Spirit of Enterprise

Economic ties constituted a very important dimension of Greek-Serb relations during the war in the former Yugoslavia. This aspect of the Greek-Serb relationship has also been, as one can easily understand, the hardest one to investigate. It has always been covered with the thickest veil of secrecy since it invariably involved violations of international law that, if made public, would seriously embarrass the Greek government and private sector.

Even today, inquiries concerning the Serb leader's reportedly considerable financial assets in Greece—in shares, bank accounts, real estate, hotels, and sailboats—are met with a wall of silence by Greek authorities. Thus, on January 28, 2001, Mladjan Dinkic, governor of the National Bank of Serbia, accused Greece, Cyprus, and Switzerland of failing to cooperate with investigators trying to trace Slobodan Milošević's secret bank accounts.

Throughout the war in the former Yugoslavia, Greece repeatedly violated the international trade embargo imposed by the UN Security Council in 1992. The massive illegalities involved not only Greek businessmen but also the Greek authorities. Greek oil companies in particular consistently violated the embargo in order to supply the Serbian war machine with much-needed fuel. In most cases, such violations occurred with the knowledge—if not the approval—of the Greek government. Even as late as 1995, when there was little doubt about the Serb and Bosnian Serb responsibility for the overwhelming majority of war crimes committed in Bosnia, Greece (and to a lesser extent Italy) continued to provide the Serb war machine with the fuel that would enable its armored vehicles to eventually roll into Srbrenica, Goražde, and other UN-designated "safe areas."

A secret European Commission report dated March, 1995, showed a pattern of continuous violations of trade sanctions by Greece. The report directly charged Greek authorities with allowing oil exports to Albania (from where it would find its way to Serbia mainly through the Lake Shkodër and the Buna River) despite the fact that "two-thirds of the fuel consignments announced from Greece were given the 'Not OK' status by Albanian authorities." In other words, Greek authorities allowed the suspect fuel consignments to be shipped to Albania without the proper clearance. That meant they were aware that the fuel was not destined for Albania, as the exporters claimed.[1]

The seaside resort of Glyfada, half an hour from the center of Athens, is not only renowned for its elegant shops and seaside restaurants, it is also the place many rich Russians—especially those who acquired their wealth after the fall of communism and are connected with the Russian Mafia—and Serbs choose to reside and as center of their financial operations. One such person was Serb multimillionaire Vladimir Bokan. The young Serb arrived in Greece in 1992 and within just two years was awarded Greek citizenship. According to a report that appeared in the French weekly *Courier International* in 1999, Bokan had been recruited by the Greek secret services to "smuggle fuel on behalf of the Mitsotakis and the Milošević governments." In exchange, the Greek government provided him with Greek citizenship and turned a blind eye to the rest of his very profitable activities, which included—apart from smuggling oil—the smuggling of cigarettes and weapons.[2]

Bokan's name started appearing in the Greek and international media in the late 1990s in association with his beautiful mansion, which allegedly belonged to Milošević's family. The Serb president's son Marko, according to these reports, had stayed at the house three years before. Moreover, according to various reports, Bokan's bank accounts in Greek and foreign banks also belonged to the Serb leader.

After trying unsuccessfully for several months to track Bokan down, I finally made contact and arranged to meet him. During the course of my interview with him in his Glyfada office in October, 2000, Bokan told me he had earned as much as $10,000 a day while breaking the international economic embargo on Yugoslavia and smuggling fuel, cigarettes, and other goods during the 1990s. It made him a multimillionaire. According to police reports appearing after his death, Bokan owned property and other assets in Greece worth tens of millions of dollars. He also ran Panama-registered and Cyprus-registered shipping companies. He "invested" his profits in Serbia. Several years ago he purchased the entire chain of kiosks in Belgrade and the northern Serbia province of Vojvoidina from the state. He also owned a chain of retail clothing stores and a real estate company in Belgrade, a ship-yard in the Danube port town of Novi Sad, a sizable share in a chemical fac-tory that produces fertilizer in Serbia, and many other holdings.

Bokan continually stressed to me that he no longer had anything to do with Milošević and that he was looking forward to a new life as a respectable businessman in the post-Milošević era in Serbia. He also said that he was in close contact with leading opposition members, including Vuk Drascovic and Zoran Djindjić.

During the course of the interview, Bokan revealed that he had been a close friend of Zeljko Ražnatovic, the late Serb paramilitary leader known as "Arkan," who had been assassinated in Belgrade in January. He told me pro-Milošević forces killed Arkan because he had grown close to Milo Djukanović, the pro-Western president of Montenegro. "Arkan wanted out," he told me. "He was starting a new life. He may even have been contemplating going to The Hague to testify."

When I asked him if he had smuggled oil to Serbia during the embargo, he readily admitted to the charge. "I did it not only for the money, but also because I wanted to help my country," he said. He said he bought a vessel in 1994 and used it to transport petroleum from the state-owned refinery in Greece to Bar in Montenegro. From there the fuel would find its way to Serbia. The Greek authorities never gave him any trouble. On the contrary, he said, they "did everything in their power to facilitate the violation of the embargo. For example, they never asked for Letters of Discharge. . . . [They] believed that the imposition of the embargo was unjust."

Bokan's revelations—which were never challenged by Greek authorities after the interview was published—were extremely important.[3] Although reports on the violation of the embargo by Greek businessmen were quite common during the 1990s, this was the first time someone directly involved revealed that Greek authorities had abetted the violations.

After the interview was over we decided to meet again. We had estab-lished a framework of trust between us. Our next discussion would focus on the ways in which various Greek businessmen and politicians help the Belgrade regime. I called him the next day—unfortunately not from a safe phone—and we arranged to meet on Tuesday, October 10. However, in the predawn hours on Saturday, October 7—five days after I had interviewed him and three days before I was supposed to meet him again—he was assassinated outside his house. According to police reports, two gunmen, one armed with a Kalashnikov submachine gun and the other with a pistol, pumped ten bullets into his head and chest. The killer or killers remain at large.

Prime Minister Andreas Papandreou and Slobodan Milošević occasionally tried to figure out ways in which their countries could bypass the UN-imposed trade embargo on Serbia. This fact emerged during a debate in the Greek Parliament concerning Greece's acquisition of four fire-fighting CL-215 airplanes from Serbia in 1995.

To get around the embargo problem, the Greek government decided to set up a company in Cyprus—which was not an EU member country—that would acquire the airplanes from Serbia and afterward sell them to Greece. Agriculture Minister Stefanos Tzoumakas accidentally revealed details of the story during the course of a June, 1997, Parliament debate in which he was trying to fend off charges of personal corruption by the opposition.

According to Tzoumakas, Prime Minister Papandreou, "after having communicated with Milošević and in cooperation with him, decided that Greece should buy four Canadair airplanes since New Yugoslavia does not need them. Well the issue is how . . . why should we buy those planes when Yugoslavia is under an embargo and a European Community member country breaks the embargo. If my opponents want this fact to be made public let it be so. It really did happen."

"In order to get around the issue of the embargo," Tzoumakas continued, "a Cypriot company was set up and through this company and with the guarantee of the Yugoslav State the transaction was made." Tzoumakas said the determination to go ahead with the plan was "a unanimous decision" made at the October 12, 1995, cabinet meeting. Nobody voiced any objection.[4]

So the deal went through. The Cypriot company, Sigman Air Support, Limited, with offices in Nicosia, purchased the planes from Serbia and "sold" them to Greece on February 5, 1997.

Some had hoped that Kostas Simitis's rise to power in 1996 would mean a radical break with the policies of his predecessor. It was expected that the new government would reveal the shady deals of its predecessor and make public the names of Greek businessmen and politicians who had made millions during the war in Bosnia. Alas, nothing happened. Indeed, the new prime minister—at least during the first year of his premiership—continued to follow faithfully in his predecessor's steps and promoted a number of Greek-Serb/Bosnian Serb agreements of a questionable nature.

One such deal involved Greece's state-owned telecommunications company (OTE). In March, 1966, OTE officials decided to start discussions with the Bosnian Serbs concerning the reconstruction of their telephone network. In May, OTE gave the Serbs a "master plan" for that network worth four hundred thousand marks and began negotiating how OTE would profit by putting the plan into effect.

The OTE officials did not show any eagerness to inform the public or their Greek and foreign shareholders of the agreement. Nor did they inform the international organizations responsible for the reconstruction of Bosnia-Herzegovina or the government of the country. They probably suspected—and rightly so—that the agreement did not harmonize with the spirit of the Dayton accords, which envisaged a united Bosnia-Herzegovina.

The OTE-planned networks would provide links between the Bosnian Serbs and Belgrade but none with the rest of Bosnia-Herzegovina. This plan was different from the European Union scheme, which envisaged three linked independent networks and not a totally separate one for the Serbs.

The Bosnian Serbs did not seem to share their Greek donor's inhibitions about revealing the plan. On May 8, 1996, *Glas Sprski,* a Bosnian-Serb newspaper published in Zvornik, announced the agreement with OTE to its readers. At the same time, it carried a rather controversial statement attributed to the leader of the Greek delegation: "This plan will enable you to gain independence from the other entity, the Muslim-Croat Federation." No one from the OTE delegation or the Greek government issued a denial at the time.

But this was not the only embarrassing point. Even more worrisome were the military implications of the agreement. The "master plan" included provisions for information transmission centers and command and control centers that could become a military threat to the rest of Bosnia in the event hostilities resumed. In the past, the Karadzic regime had rejected offers by international organizations to carry out the plan precisely because it would have to include such sensitive items.

The director of the Serbian Republic's Post Telegraph and Telephone Company (PTT) revealed all of this in a speech. He declared that the reasons Greece was chosen over other Western companies was because the Greek plan included sensitive items of a military nature that could not be revealed to the infidels.

"In the past," *Glas Sprski* quoted the official, "the representatives of the international community promised us that the European Bank for Reconstruction and Development would finance the 'master plan.' But we realized that it was up to us to find those we wanted to help us. We chose our Greek friends because we could not entrust such important information concerning our telecommunications to the first person that came along."

When the story broke a few weeks later, the international community's reaction was swift. Carl Bildt, the EU implementation chief for Bosnia-Herzegovina, protested to the Greek government that the agreement was "cutting off Sarajevo."

The reaction of the government of Bosnia-Herzegovina was predictably strong. Nedzad Hadžimusić, the Bosnian ambassador to the EU, told me that his government was "astonished that a friendly country with which we have established diplomatic relations could enter into such an agreement on such a sensitive issue without consulting the central government. This action does not promote the success of the Dayton agreement but on the contrary strengthens the separatist tendencies of the Karadzic regime."[5]

Finally, a senior EU official in the Commission's External Relations Directorate, speaking on the condition of anonymity, expressed his "regret" that Greece was channeling aid to the indicted war criminal Radovan Karadjić's government.

European Union officials had ample reason to complain. Insofar as OTE was benefiting from community largess in the form of a "crash program" designed to modernize OTE technologically and managerially, one would have expected greater sensitivity on the part of Greece's state-owned communications company to the feelings in Brussels. The fact that the concept of a "master plan," first introduced by OTE during the "crash program," would be used to secure the ethnic purity of the Bosnian-Serb circuits could hardly have been expected to improve Greece's image among its EU partners.

The Greek Ministry of Foreign Affairs dismissed the affair as a tempest in a teacup, and Foreign Affairs Minister Theodoros Pangalos appealed once again to Greek public's penchant for conspiracy theories by attributing the incident to undefined "conflicts of economic interests." On the other hand, OTE was obliged to acknowledge that it had entered into the agreement with the Bosnian Serbs without the knowledge of the international community. At the same time, OTE officials rejected the accusation that the agreement violated the Dayton accords. They also denied having made any of the statements attributed to them in *Glas Sprski*.

Kosovo

CHAPTER 5

Hating the "Franks"

In many ways, the scene in Athens during the days leading up to President Clinton's October, 1999, visit was strangely reminiscent of Belgrade during the recent NATO air campaign: the burning in effigy of the American president, the daily demonstrations against the United States, the unceasing tirades against the "NATO Killers," the graffiti denouncing the "murderers of the peoples"—all the elements that constituted the daily ritual in Belgrade also defined the corresponding daily ritual in Athens. Moreover, in both places demonstrators were burning American flags while carrying red flags that represented Serbia.[1]

There were differences, of course: The massive outpouring of anti-Western resentment in Athens was taking place in a country that was not being bombed and which also happened to be a member of both NATO and the EU. Another difference concerned the level of violence. The day President Clinton arrived in Athens, the violent confrontations between demonstrators and riot police surpassed by far the violence seen in any recent anti-American demonstration anywhere else in the world (with the possible exception of demonstrations in Tehran during the Ayatollah Khomeini era).

According to United Press International, as President Clinton was declaring how he "looked forward to experiencing that wonderful quality of Greek hospitality, demonstrators were throwing firebombs and lobbing chunks of concrete through back windows. Downtown Athens was littered with glass from broken windows, particularly banks, a favorite target of demonstrators who uprooted concrete planters to hurl through the windows."[2]

The security measures were unprecedented for a politician traveling to a supposedly friendly country. Thousands of Greek policemen lined the streets along the U.S. president's travel routes, leaving a large section of downtown Athens deserted, with all traffic banned and police standing guard behind barricades.

Some blamed the reactions on the unfortunate timing of the American president's visit, namely the fact that it coincided with the anniversary of the student uprising against the U.S.-supported military junta that had ruled Greece from 1967 to 1974. Yet not only was Bill Clinton not responsible for the U.S. policies during that period, he also was a vocal critic of the Nixon administration and its support of the colonels' regime.[3]

Although Greek authorities claimed the demonstrations were the work of an extreme fringe group, the media and public opinion polls tell a different story. "Criminal, pervert, murderer, impostor, bloodthirsty, gangster slayer, criminal, butcher, stupid, killer, foolish, unscrupulous, dishonest, disgraceful, rascal." were just some of the adjectives used to describe Clinton by the overwhelming majority of Greek media.[4] Meanwhile, opinion polls taken before the president's arrival showed that 61 percent of respondents wanted Clinton's visit postponed, whereas only 24 percent welcomed it. The national daily, *Ta Nea,* reported that foreign diplomats and correspondents said "Athens is the most anti-American European capital."[5] French

10. School children in Athens demonstrate against the NATO attack on Serbia in the spring of 1999. Photo courtesy Eleftherotypia.

11. A demonstration in Athens against NATO's air campaign against Serbia in the spring of 1999. Photo courtesy Eleftherotypia.

sociologist Edgar Morin, who was visiting Athens during Clinton's visit, characterized what was going on as "fundamental irrationalism."[6]

The event that seemed to have served as the main catalyst for reawakening the most virulent form of anti-American sentiment in recent years was NATO's bombing of Serbia. The protests against President Clinton were, in many ways, a continuation and culmination of the daily mass outpourings of hatred for NATO and "American imperialism" that took place in Athens during the Kosovo war. According to opinion polls published during that period, 96–98 percent of the Greek public opposed the NATO air campaign.

No other event had been able to unleash more the pent-up frustrations of the Greek psyche than the events in neighboring Kosovo. Stronger even than the mass hysteria the country witnessed in the early 1990s over the Macedonia issue, this collective outpouring of emotions gave rise to an anti-Western and anti-American rhetoric of hate unthinkable for a modern European country.

From the very outset of the war, the Greek Orthodox Church, led by telegenic Archbishop Christodoulos, adopted a strong anti-Western rhetoric while closely identifying with its Serbian "brethren." The leader of the Greek Church not only voiced his "complete solidarity with the heroic Orthodox Serb people," he also condemned the air strikes as "a brutal violation of ideals and principles of democracy and freedom by the mighty of the earth that have unleashed the storm."[7]

The archbishop saw in the Western intervention in Kosovo "an attempt to eliminate the Orthodox element from every corner of Europe."[8] Repeating standard Serb propaganda claims, he claimed that Kosovo was the cradle of the Serb nation, and that NATO's attacks, while being carried out "under the pretext of trying to impose justice," in reality "aimed to exterminate the Serbs."[9] According to Christodoulos, the aim of NATO and the West was not only to exterminate the Serbs but also to eliminate their religious monuments. Speaking at the Saint Panteleimon Church in Athens, the archbishop referred to the "hate against Orthodoxy" that presumably motivated the NATO attacks. He then went on to state that "the target of the attacks were the Orthodox monasteries" in the region.[10]

Not wanting to be outdone, Archbishop Chrysostomos of Cyprus alleged that the Jewish lobby in the United States had played a role in prompting the NATO campaign against Serbia.[11]

In a sense, the unfolding drama constituted a replay of what went on before during the war in Bosnia. What was especially intriguing about the Greek reaction was not so much the expressions of solidarity with the innocent Serb victims of the NATO bombings, but the total lack of concern for the plight of the Albanian Kosovars. Once again, the victims of Serb aggression were totally ignored by Greek society.

Dignitaries of the Greek Orthodox Church in particular seemed oblivious to the suffering of the Kosovar Albanians before and during the war. At best they showed feelings of utter indifference for the suffering of the hundred of thousands of Albanian refugees. At worst one could occasionally find statements revealing an extreme inhumanity. This was the case, for example, with some of the statements made by Archbishop Christodoulos. When asked if he thought Greece should take in refugees from Kosovo he said: "Who created the armies of refugees? Those who are responsible should also take care of them."[12] This, of course, implied that the responsibility belonged to the Western powers, which, according to the typical Greek view, were responsible for creating the refugee problem. The majority of Greeks shared the archbishop's opinion concerning the fate of the Kosovo refugees. A poll taken during that period revealed that 52 percent of Greeks were against the admittance into the country of fleeing Albanian refugees.[13]

Throughout the conflict in Kosovo not a single party protested the Serb atrocities, not a single protest was made to the Yugoslav embassy, not a single open-air concert was held in support of the fleeing Albanians. Instead, demonstrators marched daily on the U.S. embassy in Athens and sloganeers focused on framing the United States and NATO as "murderers." In a similar vein, outdoor concerts held in Athens during the period sought to express the support of the Greek people for the suffering Serbs. At the same time, a continuous stream of well-known intellectuals—academics, lawyers, and so forth—traveled to Belgrade to protest "U.S. imperialism" and to express solidarity with their Orthodox Serb brethren.[14]

Popular outrage was carefully channeled in one direction: toward NATO, the West, and the United States. The Kosovo Albanians were totally blocked out of the Greek vision. In April, twenty judges from Greece's highest administrative court announced that NATO was committing war crimes by violating Serbia's sovereignty. No mention was made of the human rights violations the Serb government was committing against the Albanians.[15]

Visiting foreigners expressed dismay and incomprehension at the Greek reactions. "Why," wondered Bjorn Roe, a visiting Norwegian scholar, "are the Greeks not willing to see the unjust suffering of the Kosovo people who have been harassed, have lost their freedom of expression and have been bombed and killed by the thousands?"[16]

Karin Hope, the *Economist*'s correspondent in Athens, witnessed an incident that highlighted the lack of sensitivity to the plight of the Albanian Kosovars. On the morning of March 30, 1999, she went to the foreign ministry's elegant neoclassical building on Vasilissis Sofias Avenue to interview George Papandreou. She explained in English to the two male receptionists why she was there, and one telephoned the minister's office while the other turned around and resumed watching television. She looked to see what he found so absorbing. It was a CNN report from Macedonia showing a group of ethnic Albanians clutching children and suitcases stumbling down a steep wooded hillside. His eyes still glued to the screen, the receptionist said fiercely: "Those people aren't human beings. They are animals." "That's right," said his smartly dressed colleague as he put down the phone. "That's what they are!"[17]

The NATO alliance was portrayed as a criminal gang bent on destroying innocent lives. The leaders of the Western nations—Blair and Clinton in particular—were portrayed as cold-blooded executioners, and most newspapers daily carried at least one commentary in which President Clinton was compared to Adolf Hitler.

Even the Greek security apparatus decided to join the "anti-imperialist Front." The Greek policemen's union issued a declaration stating that "the police refuse to be used as guards for the NATO troops that are landing in our country and are being sent to neighboring Yugoslavia where they may be used against the suffering people of Serbia."[18] On March 2, Greek soldiers and sailors joined in a demonstration followed by a march to the American embassy in Athens despite the fact that it is illegal in Greece for members of the armed forces to participate in any kind of political activity. The few hundred service personnel who took part in the march were fully aware that they risked being arrested and court-martialed for their action.[19]

The picture of the war in Kosovo emerging from the Greek media was totally different from the one that predominated in the West. It was as if there were two different wars. The editorial positions taken by the overwhelming majority in the Greek media during the period of the NATO bombings had little, if anything, in common with those of their Western counterparts. The main difference from the very start concerned the attribution of blame. All the Greek newspapers—without exception—blamed NATO and the United States for the outbreak of the hostilities.

On March 24, the day hostilities commenced, *Ta Nea,* Greece's largest daily (a left-of-center publication) asserted that although the NATO raids against Serbia were supposed to settle the Kosovo crisis, in reality their aim was "to end the civil strife with a victory for the Albanian autonomists." Greece's second largest daily, *Eleftherotypia* (a Leftist paper) ran a story under the headline "Clinton strikes and the UN collapses" in which it argued that the aim of the NATO air campaign was to confirm American monocracy. The United States, according to *Eleftherotypia,* "considers legitimate whatever serves its interests." The intervention in Kosovo represented nothing more than another step in U.S. efforts to attain world hegemony. The conservative newspaper *Kathimerini* justified Belgrade's refusal to sign the Rambouillet agreement. Had Belgrade allowed the introduction of NATO forces, the paper argued, it would have lost control over Kosovo, which would then gradually move toward secession from Serbia. That was something no ruler and no country could accept. "The way the West has handled the issue," *Kathimerini* concluded, "indicates that it doesn't seek a viable compromise solution but that it seeks instead Serbia's humiliation."

The less serious dailies adopted an even stronger anti-Western rhetoric. Front-page headlines in *Adesmeftos Tipos* (conservative) informed its readership that the "US and NATO plan a third Balkan war," while *Apogevmatini*'s (conservative) headlines revealed there were "Turkish soldiers on our borders to protect Albania from Greece." Another conservative daily, *Vradini,* announced that a "Balkan Storm has started: The international butcher [Clinton] has given the green light for a massacre."

In his study of the Greek media, London *Times* correspondent John Carr mentions that some of the Greek journalists he interviewed spoke of "editorial terrorism" to describe the fact that both during the Bosnia war as well as during the NATO strikes on Serbia in 1999 "Greek opinion-molders were expected to be knee-jerk pro-Serb."[20]

In many cases, the Albanians were portrayed as fleeing not because they were being expelled by the Serbs (the view in the West) but because of NATO bombings. In a similar vein, the local media attributed the mass destruction of property in Kosovo to the NATO bombings, whereas the Western media claimed the Serbs were burning their victims out. From the first night of hostilities, Greek television stations started transmitting footage that purported to portray NATO air attacks against Pristina. In reality, the first NATO rocket did not hit Pristina until a week after the air attacks on Yugoslavia were initiated.

The anti-Western editorial stance adopted by the overwhelming majority in the Greek media also influenced the ranking of news items. The Greek media's coverage of the war in Kosovo constantly underplayed accusations of Serb atrocities and the mass exodus of Albanians. The mass expulsion of hundreds of thousands of ethnic Albanian refugees from Kosovo rarely, if ever, got headline coverage in any of the twenty or so national dailies. The front-page headlines were in most cases reserved for the victims of "NATO aggression."

In his study of the Greek media during the Kosovo war, German sociologist Gustav Auernheimer mentions two additional instances of questionable reporting. During at least the first weeks of the war, Greek television stations uncritically aired Serb television footage without mentioning the source. This was crucial because it meant that the Greek audience was exposed to Serb propaganda (for example, allegations that NATO planes were purposely attacking civilian targets).

Another instance Auernheimer mentions is the coverage of the murder of Serb journalist Slavko Čuruvija, a vocal critic of the Milošević regime, on April 11. The incident was barely reported in the Greek media, which was preoccupied with showing how the Serbs were celebrating Easter.[21]

That Greek media coverage had very little in common with that of the Western media was also testified to by some of the letters sent by members of Athens's foreign community to the *Athens News*, an English-language daily. "How," wrote one reader, "can Greeks believe that the Kosovars are fleeing the bombings when there is so much evidence to show that the Serbs have . . . driven them out of their houses?"[22] Another reader questioned the whole coverage of the war: "Everything that we have read in the Greek press and seen on the Greek television is blatantly pro-Serbian and shows a very limited understanding of the humanitarian aims of NATO involvement in Kosovo. In fact, it reveals a people and a press steeped in hatred, prejudice and fear who will be unable to move forward in the new Europe that is emerging. The Greeks are driven by loathing of everything American and Muslim to the extent of paranoia."[23] A third reader wrote: "Having lived in Greece for the past three years I am truly astonished by both its media and its people's reaction to the NATO campaign against the Milošević regime. I am told that Greek people are warm, caring, family-oriented people but this is only toward their own Orthodox kin and clearly to the detriment of ethnic Albanians and their families."[24]

Of course, not everybody shared these critical views. Archbishop Christodoulos was ecstatic with the coverage: "In Greece, journalists have proven once again that they are true Greeks and Christians."[25]

Progovernment Serb journalists were equally ecstatic with the Greek media. In an interview with the Greek daily *Eleftherotypia,* Nebojša Djordić, editor of the progovernment *Politika,* when asked to explain the fact that Greek journalists' coverage of the war differed significantly from that of their Western colleagues, attributed it to the fact that the Greeks had not become as "alienated" or "brainwashed" as the rest of the Europeans. "The people of the Mediterranean and of the Balkans have not as yet become robots," he said. "We listen very often to the dictates of our heart and our soul. We reject the prefabricated ways of the American model."[26]

Particularly controversial were the journalistic practices adopted by the contingent of Greek correspondents the Serbs had allowed to remain in Pristina. The Greek journalists (with the exception of one Turk and one American) were the only ones—from a press corps that prior to the NATO action numbered approximately one hundred journalists—the Serbs allowed to remain in Kosovo. The Greek journalists remaining in Kosovo were criticized for having agreed to present a picture of the situation that conformed to the wishes of the Serb authorities in exchange for being allowed to stay. Their response was that war reporting had its own rules. The main objective was to be able to stay at the "scene of the crime" even if that involved some relaxation of the journalistic ethics of fair and accurate reporting.[27]

The most serious charges were leveled by Greek journalist Christos Tellidis, one of the oldest and most experienced Greek Balkan correspondents. According to Tellidis, who was in Pristina when the war started, the behavior of the Greek journalists allowed to remain went against all the rules of journalistic reporting.[28]

Specifically, Tellidis reported the following:

1. That while eighty or so foreign colleagues were being expelled from Kosovo, Greek journalists pleaded with Serb authorities to be allowed to stay.
2. That Greek journalists participated with Serb troops in the attacks on Albanian villages. "My colleagues from a Greek television station," he wrote, "showed us with some pride shots that they had taken while sitting on the top of Serb tanks. The tanks were smashing through Albanian villages not only to attack the UCK but also Kosovar civilians." The Greek journalists avoided mentioning in their reporting the Serb human rights violations they had observed.
3. That Greek journalists were consciously and consistently transmitting footage that had no bearing on reality. For example, when the attack on Serbia commenced at 9 p.m. on March 24, Greek television reporters were transmitting footage that purportedly showed Pristina being hit by NATO bombs. Yet not a single rocket had hit the city. In one case, Greek stations showed footage of a building on fire while the reporter informed viewers that a NATO rocket had hit it. In reality, it was the building that housed the Albanian newspaper *Kosovo Today* and witnesses testified that Serbs set it on fire. In another case, Greek television reported that a rocket targeting the building housing a Pristina radio and TV station missed its target and instead hit a nearby Serbian house, causing a lot of damage. Once again this was not the case. Explosive devices placed by Serbs destroyed the house, which was located in an Albanian neighborhood.

Tellidis also mentioned that the Kosovo Albanians developed very negative feelings toward the Greek journalists. I was able confirm this when I visited the camps at Stankovac in Macedonia, where the majority of the Albanian refugees from Kosovo were living. I could sense among the refugees distrust bordering on contempt for Greek journalists. They were seen as parts of the Serb propaganda machine. What seemed to irk them most was what they perceived as a total lack of concern by the Greeks for the suffering of the local Albanian population. "Why are you supporting what the Serbs are doing to us? Why are you lying?" were the most common questions I encountered while trying to talk to them.[29]

Those feelings were very clearly expressed by Marin Kaidoncay, an Albanian UNHCR officer in Pristina, in a letter published in the Athens daily *Eleftherotypia*. In it, Kaidoncay recalled how on Sunday, March 28, four days after the bombing started, while he was in his way to his office in the area of Dragovar, he was arrested by three Serb policemen who forced him to the ground and started kicking and beating him with wooden clubs:

> Suddenly two cars with television cameras approached us carrying approximately 6–8 people. The cars stopped while the journalists inside watched the scene that was unfolding in front of their eyes. Then they continued their drive and stopped 100 meters farther down the road. The cars and the television equipment carried visible Greek insignia. Meanwhile, the policemen continued beating me, with the result that they broke my left hand and arm as well as two ribs. Throughout this incident the journalists did not try to film what was going on or to interfere in any way. When the policemen got tired of beating me they left, leaving me bleeding on the ground. I got up slowly and started making my way in the direction of a friend of mine who had come with his car to pick me up. I passed in front of the journalists who at the time were filming a queue in front of a bakery. Once again they saw me and ignored me.[30]

One of the most interesting aspects of the massive anti-Western mobilization that took place in Greece during the Kosovo war was its intolerance. There was very little space for dissent even in the mildest of forms. Total conformity with the feelings and views of the "masses" was demanded from individuals, journalists, and institutions alike. This climate of opinion affected, first and foremost, some institutions of civil society that collapsed like a house of cards. If "civil society" is understood, as young Karl Marx argued in his "On the Jewish Question," as the place where individuality and difference reign supreme, then this place very soon dissolved into an amorphous mass that was rioting in the streets against NATO, burning U.S. flags and attacking Western embassies.

The collapse of civil society manifested itself in the fact that some humanitarian NGOs, responding to the pressure of public opinion, found themselves directly or indirectly supporting Milošević's regime. The most celebrated instance concerned the Greek chapter of the organization Doctors Without Borders (DWB). Its case became internationally known after the parent organization decided to expel the Greek chapter from its ranks on June 12, 1999. Not only was the decision unprecedented in the history of the organization, it was made unanimously by the other eighteen national chapters.

The Greek DWB chapter was accused of collaborating with the Belgrade regime despite the fact that the Serb government had banned the parent organization from entering Kosovo. According to Philippe Biberson, president of the French DWB chapter, the Greek chapter "violated the norms of political impartiality of the organization" and "the Greek doctors had direct consultation with the government of Belgrade and with the Greek embassy"—something that was "explicitly forbidden by the organization."[31] James Orbinski, international president of DWB, added that the Greeks "held non-impartial and non-objective positions." Moreover, he concluded, "They made declarations favorable to the Serbs and unfavorable to the Albanians who were the victims of ethnic cleansing."[32]

Responding to criticism from the Greek chapter that the DWB was more interested in the fate of Albanians than of Serbs, DWB general secretary Jean Marie Kindermans said: "Of course we wanted to organize humanitarian missions in Serbia, but the Milošević regime refused to give us visas. There existed no guarantees securing the independence and impartiality of the mission. So we decided that we could not intervene in Serbia. It was a common decision. In addition, there was the issue of ethnic cleansing and of crimes against humanity in Kosovo."[33]

The reactions in Greece to the DWB's decision were predictably strong. The DWB became the focus of attack by the overwhelming majority of the media, politicians, and even the government. After a session of its inner cabinet at which the issue was discussed, the government rushed to adopt the "nationally correct" position of praising the Greek chapter for its bravery and courage. The majority of the media and many politicians from all parties went much farther: They denounced not only the DWB, but also all humanitarian NGOs as being "racists," "mercenaries" of NATO or of the CIA, and "dependent on foreign interests." Nikos Mouzelis of the London School of Economics summed up the Greek reaction: "All these articles in the Greek media which present the DWB and the committee that awarded them the Nobel Peace Prize as instruments of NATO and the US, convey less information about these organizations and more about the completely paranoid character of Greek nationalism—a nationalism that sees everywhere conspiracies against the Chosen People, who are always right and who are constantly abused by the mighty of the world."[34]

As far as the Greek government was concerned, its policies were once again marked by its inability to articulate an argument that would put at the forefront the human rights tragedy that had been unfolding in Kosovo during the years prior to and during the NATO intervention.

This was no accident. The official policy of Andreas Papandreou's PASOK government, whose ideological-political legacy Prime Minister Kostas Simitis inherited, constituted an explicit endorsement of Slobodan Milošević's repression in Kosovo. Papandreou laid out this policy in a revealing and systematic manner in a 1993 article in *Ta Nea* in which he outlined the policy his government would follow upon returning to power.[35]

Papandreou argued that any plan to put Kosovo under UN supervision would lead to the destabilization of the region: "The presence of U.S. and NATO troops will encourage the Albanians to revolt against the Serbs." He argued that Albanian president Sali Berisha and "especially Muslim countries like Saudi Arabia and Turkey" were promoting this destabilization. The Greek leader totally accepted Serbian propaganda claims concerning the region: "Kosovo was the cradle of the Serb civilization and their Jerusalem. If a war breaks out in Kosovo the Serbs will fight to the last man or woman or child to prevent this area from gaining independence."

It is noteworthy that throughout the article, the PASOK leader did not once mention the repressive regime the Serbs had instituted in Kosovo, or the abolition of Kosovo's autonomy by Belgrade at the end of the 1980s. The whole of Papandreou's article reaffirmed the existing status quo. "Do not touch Kosovo," he concluded. "Otherwise we will all go up in flames."

Moreover, Papandreou never mentioned in the article, let alone discussed, the demands made by moderate Albanian leader Ibrahim Rugova. In a sense, Papandreou appeared to be even more of a hard-liner than Slobodan Milošević, who at least acknowledged the existence of some "problems" and that the Albanians had some "legitimate demands."

The only fresh idea that Papandreou offered in his article was that placing UN forces between Albania and Kosovo might diffuse the coming crisis. In other words, the future prime minister of Greece was asking the UN to guarantee the illegal status quo brought about by Milošević's abolition of the region's autonomy.

There was no discernible change in Greece's policy of accommodation during the early years of Prime Minister Kostas Simitis's government.[36] As late as 1998, the Greek Foreign Ministry was encouraging Greek firms to invest in Serb-run enterprises in Kosovo despite the strong protests of Ibrahim Rugova and the outlawed Albanian trade unions.[37] At the same time, some government ministers were implicated in questionable dealings with members of Belgrade's underworld who were also involved in the murder of Albanian Kosovo activists in Europe.[38]

An incident involving Minister of Foreign Affairs Theodoros Pangalos underlined the support Milošević continued to enjoy from the Greek side. The incident took place during a conference on Kosovo organized in January, 1998, by ELIAMEP, a Greek think tank. "I had just made a speech," recalled Dr. Dušan Janić, the Serb director of an NGO group in Belgrade, "in which I argued that Greece and the international community should suggest to Mr. Milošević a 'Pinochet solution.' Namely that he should step down from power and in exchange be declared something like senator for life or something similar. No sooner had I finished making the proposal than I saw Greece's foreign minister, Theodoros Pangalos, his face red with rage, screaming at me: 'I will never do such a thing to my friend Milošević. I will never betray my friend!'"[39]

Former ND Party Trade and Industry Minister Andreas Andrianopoulos argued that the government had failed during the first week of the conflict to justify the alliance's decision to bomb Yugoslavia in order to thwart the ethnic cleansing of Kosovo Albanians. Andrianopoulos recalled that shortly after NATO planes started bombing military targets in Serbia and Montenegro none other than Defense Minister Akis Tsochatzopoulos expressed dismay at the breach of peace and reiterated his belief that a diplomatic solution was feasible. "The Greek Foreign Minister George Papandreou was no better," continued Andrianopoulos. "In a CNN interview he displayed his displeasure with the way the Serbian leader had been misunderstood by the West. And although one may have expected otherwise from the Prime Minister, Kostas Simitis publicly expressed his annoyance at Mr. Clinton's insinuation that NATO involvement may have checked possible Greek-Turkish hostilities that could have resulted if the Kosovo crisis spread south."[40]

The Greek government later tried to change its line and finally mentioned the crimes the Serbs were perpetrating against the native Albanian population. Prime Minister Kostas Simitis, Foreign Minister George Papandreou, and even Theodoros Pangalos issued strong statements condemning the atrocities Milošević's troops were committing in Kosovo. Yet when government officials were given the chance to confront the views of NATO's critics, in most cases they avoided doing so.

A very revealing incident took place in the Church of Saint Neapolis in Salonika where Archbishop Christodoulos was invited to deliver a speech. The leader of the Greek Orthodox Church referred to the American president (without naming him) as "Satan," "Demon," "insidious fascist," and "Christian only in name" for ordering the air attacks against Serbia. When Minister of Development Evangelos Venizelos took the floor after the archbishop finished his speech, he praised the archbishop for the "depth and sincerity" of his remarks.[41]

However, it is worth noting that only municipal governments carried out officially inspired anti-Western acts. This was the case with authorities in the city of Chania on Crete, who issued a statement containing veiled threats to the physical safety of U.S. military personnel at the American air base in Souda: "We the members of the local Government, being fully aware of the anger of our compatriots, would like to inform the government that the American soldiers are unwelcome here and we cannot guarantee their personal safety or whatever else may happen to them. We ask the people to boycott the American multinational companies and to refuse to have any dealings with them."[42]

Even more serious was a statement made by the prefect of Chania, George Katsanevakis, who declared that the U.S. ambassador in Athens, Nicholas Burns, was "unwelcome" on the island. This was the first time something like that had happened in a country belonging to NATO or the EU. A government spokesman condemned the prefect's statement.[43]

An important element in the reactions to the war in Kosovo was terrorism directed against Western targets. According to the U.S. State Department, from March to May, 1999, Western interests suffered some forty attacks. "Greece," the report asserted, "remained one of the weakest links in Europe's efforts against terrorism."[44]

One of the most serious incidents occurred in April, when a bomb placed at the Intercontinental Hotel in Athens killed one Greek citizen and injured another. Greek police defused a bomb placed outside the Rockefeller Foundation in Thessaloniki in March. Other terrorist acts involved the use of improvised explosives and on one occasion a drive-by shooting of the American library in Athens by a motorcyclist.

Only one arrest was made: an alert consulate guard caught a woman attempting to firebomb the U.S. consulate in Thessaloniki as a protest against NATO intervention in Kosovo. Her trial took place in February, 2001. She was given a five-month suspended sentence and set free.

The last and bloodiest of the Greek reactions to the war in Kosovo took place on June 8, 2000—one year after the end of the war—when Britain's senior military representative in Greece, Brigadier Stephen Saunders, was gunned down in a terrorist road ambush in central Athens. A nationalist terrorist group, "November 17," claimed responsibility for the daylight assassination. The group issued a thirteen-page communiqué saying that it killed the British diplomat because he had participated in the "planning of the barbaric air strikes" against Serbia the previous year.[45]

Over the past twenty-five years, November 17 has killed twenty-three people—including a CIA Athens station chief and three other Americans. Not a single member of the organization has ever been arrested. Since its inception, November 17 has also fired rockets at the Athens branches of Procter and Gamble, American Express, British Petroleum, Alico, Nationalen Nederlanden, IBM, Citibank, McDonalds, General Motors, Chase Manhattan, Midland, and the National Bank of Paris.[46] The group was especially active during the Kosovo war. From March to May, 1999, it carried out seven rocket attacks and bombings against Greek, American, and third country interests. November 17's targets during the Kosovo crisis included two offices of the governing PASOK Party; American, British, and French banks; and the Dutch ambassador's residence.[47]

In its thirteen-page communiqué regarding the British diplomat's murder, November 17 reproduced chapter and verse the set of "truths" that defined the discourse of the overwhelming majority of Greek public-opinion makers concerning Kosovo.[48] Those "truths" included, among other things, that the forceful eviction of Kosovo Albanians from their homes by the Serbs did not start until after the NATO bombings had begun, that no mass atrocities against Kosovo Albanians were discovered after the war ended, and that NATO consistently and intentionally struck civilian targets in Yugoslavia.

As for the causes of this "murderous imperialist war," the November 17 proclamation simply reproduced the views that dominated most of the Greek media throughout the conflict. The terrorist organization claimed that the reasons for NATO's intervention were not humanitarian but rather were related to the West's strategic and economic interests in Kosovo. Kosovo constituted an entry point to areas of prime strategic importance to the West, including Iraq, Iran, Afghanistan, and the Caucasus. It was no accident, the proclamation continued, that the Americans were building a super fortress in Kosovo.

As far as economic aspects were concerned, the communiqué accused the West of intervening in Kosovo because it wanted to exploit the area's mineral resources. Another reason the communiqué cited for bombing Serbia was the fact that the West wanted to destroy the Zastava automobile factory where the Yugo car was produced: "This was a car, although it was not advanced technologically, had nevertheless enjoyed considerable success even in the U.S. insofar as it targeted low-income groups." The November 17 group said that because they were unable to compete with the Yugo's low price in the marketplace, Western automobile manufacturers demanded NATO flatten the Yugo factory with cruise missiles.

November 17's declaration faithfully reproduced the Greek media's interpretation of events in Kosovo and its reporting style. The group's communiqué thus was sprinkled with references to "NATO's barbaric acts," to "Nazi crimes against Yugoslavia," and to "Hitler's bombing"—phrases that could have been taken directly from the headlines in most Greek newspapers.

The popular reaction to Brigadier Saunders's murder was once again muted. Although few Greeks sympathize with the violent methods November 17 employed, there is certainly a partial to total overlap (depending on the issue) between the worldview of November 17 and that of broad sections of the Greek population. This is attested to by, among other things, the fact that in a country where street demonstrations and protests are quite common, not a single rally has ever been staged against terrorism during the past two decades. This contrasts sharply with the situation in Spain and Italy, where the major political forces have repeatedly led demonstrations expressing solidarity with the victims and demanding action against the terrorists. There has been no such outcry in Greece.

November 17 has in most cases selected lines of action that could be ideologically legitimized by reference to widely held beliefs among the Greek population. Attacks against American targets have been justified as acts of resistance against the "conspiracies" of "U.S. imperialism"; attacks against Turkish diplomats by reference to the long history of enmity between the two countries; the targeting of foreign enterprises by reference to the sinister activities of evil multinationals; and attacks against Greek business people and industrialists by appeals to anticapitalist sentiments.[49] However, none of the previous attacks—with the exception perhaps of the assassination of some junta torturers in the mid-1970s—commanded such a strong and widespread ideological legitimacy as the attack against the British military attaché.

Every item in the terrorist group's proclamation had previously appeared in the Greek news media. The leading opinion makers of Greek society had previously voiced every argument against the Kosovo war. It would by no means be an overstatement to claim that—at least on issues like Kosovo, Bosnia, NATO, and the United States—views similar to those voiced by the terrorists reflected and continue to reflect the overwhelming majority of the Greek mass media.

CHAPTER 6

A Very Special Relationship

The young police officer had no idea of the magnitude of his catch on that hot day in July, 1995. He thought the blond man with the strange English accent lying on a beach in Rhodes that he had just arrested was simply another tourist wanted for disorderly behavior. Had he known who the foreigner was, he probably would never have dared to make the arrest in the first place. The man was none other than Darko Ansanin, the undisputed leader of Belgrade's underworld. His specialty was protecting car smugglers operating in eastern Serbia. He was also a very successful entrepreneur who owned several casinos around the country. His Belgrade casino was a meeting place for artists and gamblers like Bosnian Serb leader Radovan Karadzic, who used to frequent the place.

There was another side to Ansanin, however. He reputedly worked for Slobodan Milošević's secret police in a very sensitive area: Organizing and occasionally carrying out the executions of people the regime considered a nuisance.

This double role as a member of the underworld on one hand and a state-employed assassin on the other was not unusual in Belgrade in the 1990s. On the contrary, state security agencies often turned to underworld figures to do their dirty work—especially killing Kosovo Albanians engaged in anti-Serb activities around Europe.

According to Božidar Spačić, who spent twenty-five years as a member of Serbia's Federal State Security and from 1980 was the first inspector responsible for "special assignments," the use of these elements by the secret services began in 1972. He said he never paid a killer more than $5,000. The majority of the killers, he added, carried out their assignments not only for reasons of "national interest" but also in order to obtain false passports from the security services.

"I issued ninety false passports," Spačić boasted. " I also gave the best of them a driver's license. I once gave a passport to a restaurant owner in Geneva who executed an assignment for us in Switzerland. We met in Trieste and I gave him a Coca-Cola can containing an explosive device. As soon as he reached Geneva he threw it at a group of Albanian protesters. We also gave a passport to Matić, who must be congratulated for the operation he carried out against Javid Halintai, an Albanian whose house we destroyed."[1]

The young officer in Rhodes knew nothing of all this. He had merely been following the orders of his superiors at the police precinct, who in turn were acting on the basis of a message they had received from Interpol requesting the immediate arrest of the Serb.

Ansanin was suspected of having murdered a Kosovar Albanian human rights activist in February, 1990, in Brussels, and Belgian authorities had issued an arrest warrant. The message was accompanied by Ansanin's passport number (it was a fake passport, of course) and photograph. Had the young officer from Rhodes known all this, he probably would have walked away. Had he done so, he probably would have saved his superiors at the Greek Ministry of Justice and perhaps even higher considerable embarrassment. But he did not, and in so doing he started the ball rolling in the saga of what became known as the "Ansanin case."

Ansanin was imprisoned in Rhodes, and on October 17 the Belgian government officially requested the Serb's extradition. The Greek Supreme Court decided in favor of his extradition to Belgium in December. The case seemed closed and sealed. In a couple of days, Ansanin would board a plane that would take him to Brussels. Or so everybody thought.

At the last minute, the invisible hand of the Greek-Serbian "special relationship" once again intervened. Darko Ansanin knew too many things concerning the Serb regime's activities. He knew especially too much about the "killer-squads" that targeted ethnic Albanian activists in Europe. Equally important, he also knew too much about the shady operations some Greek businessmen were engaged in with their Serb counterparts.

Leonidas Chatziprodromidis tells the following story, which is indicative of the ties that bound Ansanin to Greek businessmen:

Once, while on a business visit in Belgrade, the Greek representative of an export firm asked the general director of his company's Serb trading partner what security measures his company should take to avoid having its merchandise shipments stolen. The Serb, who was also a member of Milošević's Socialist Party, told him not to worry. He said he would take him that night to meet somebody who would guarantee the safety of his goods. When evening came they drove to Ansanin's house and were invited in. Ansanin took the Greek visitor by the arm and led him to a back room filled with a wide variety of guns and ammunition. "I guarantee everything," he said, grinning broadly. "You have nothing to worry about."[2]

An ingenious plan was devised to help Ansanin avoid his extradition to Brussels. The plan reportedly was the brainchild of Yugoslav ambassador Milan Milutinović, who later became Serbia's prime minister and was subsequently indicted by the War Crimes Tribunal for his role in Kosovo. In any case, the plan was well received in Athens because it allowed Greek authorities to retain their "very special relationship" with Milošević's regime while at the same time saving them from embarrassing revelations.

Following the master plan, Ansanin's Belgrade lawyer, Tom Fila (a Serb of Greek descent), cooperated with the public prosecutor, who charged Ansanin with the murder of a nonexistent person. "It must have been the first court case in history," observed Chatziprodromidis, "in which the public prosecutor and defense attorney conspired to charge somebody with a crime he did not commit and thus relieve him of the charges for a crime he did commit!"[3]

On January 10, 1996, a lower court in Belgrade issued an arrest warrant for Ansanin on the trumped up charge of premeditated murder. Yugoslav authorities notified the Greek government that same day, and on January 14, the Greek minister of justice signed off on Darko Ansanin's extradition to Belgrade. Having refrained from making a decision for an entire month after the Greek Supreme Court's decision to extradite Ansanin to Belgium, it took the Greek minister of justice only four days to comply with the decision of a lower court in Belgrade.

Ansanin's lawyer in Greece, Alexandros Lykourezos (whose clients include indicted war criminal Ratco Mladić) was ecstatic: "We achieved a miracle," the Belgrade weekly *Vreme* quoted him as saying. Ansanin arrived in Belgrade on January 25 and, after spending a week in prison, he was set free. The charges against him were dropped, the trial forgotten, and he was soon pursuing his profitable activities.

The Belgian ambassador in Athens, whom I met after Ansanin's departure, could not believe what had happened. He was, of course, aware of the "very special relationship" that existed between Greece and Milošević's Serbia. However, he could not believe that this special connection extended to helping

Belgrade's gangsters escape international justice. His state of mind was reflected in the very undiplomatic language he used to describe the Greek government's actions: "The Belgian government feels deeply distressed and disappointed by the way it has been tricked by the Greek government."[4]

A Serbian opposition newspaper reported that Greece gave in to Serb demands for two reasons. The first was money. According to the paper, Greek authorities received DM 3 million to set Ansanin free. The second was threats. Belgrade made it clear to the Greeks that if they extradited the Serb secret agent to Belgium, the Serb government would make public various aspects of Greek involvement in the war in Yugoslavia that would seriously embarrass the Greek government in the eyes of its Western allies.[5] It is noteworthy that the Greek government never challenged the revelations, nor did it sue the paper for its allegations.

Darko Ansanin did not live long enough to enjoy the full fruits of his labor. On June 30, 1998, two years after his departure from Greece, he was gunned down in the fashionable Dedinje area in Belgrade. By then the Serb capital had been plagued by a series of gangland killings in which he played a prominent role. His killer or killers remain unknown, but it is likely that many must have felt greatly relieved by his death.

Judging from Ansanin's past record as well as the lengths to which Serb authorities went to avoid having him extradited to Belgium, it would not be unreasonable to assume that he played an important role in the operations Belgrade's security forces carried out against ethnic Albanian activists from Kosovo. Had Greece handed Ansanin over to Belgium, these networks would probably have been exposed. One can only speculate on the reasons for Greece's unwillingness to cooperate with its European partners.

One of the most interesting manifestations of the Greek-Serbian "special relationship" concerned the Trepća mines in Kosovo. The story of Greek involvement in those mines constitutes a prime example of the close collaboration that existed between the Greek state and Greek business on one hand and the Milošević regime on the other. At the same time, the Trepća episode also highlighted the lack of sensitivity exhibited by the Greek side toward Kosovo's Albanian population and its elected leaders.

The heart of the story is the Trepća mines, the most "expensive piece of real estate in the Balkans," as British journalist Robert Fisk has so aptly termed it.[6] The area is a mother lode of lead, cadmium, gold, silver, chromium, manganese, copper, and other ores. The enterprise known as Trepća is a conglomerate of forty mines and factories located mostly in Kosovo but also in other locations in Serbia and Montenegro.[7] Its activities include chemical processing and production of goods as varied as batteries and paint. But the heart of its operations and the source of most of its raw materials is the vast mining complex to the east of Mitrovica in northern Kosovo.

Beginning in 1974, when Tito's new constitution accorded the province autonomy, Kosovo acquired considerable control over the resources of the province. However, after Tito's death, Belgrade reasserted its control of the mines and from 1981–89 monopolized the export of Trepća minerals to Russia and elsewhere, reaping the profits in hard currency and oil while compensating the Kosovars with electricity and other nonfungible forms of payment. At that time the mines were still under ethnic Albanian management. By the late 1980s, however, with their final integration into the Serbian power-generating system, Kosovars had lost virtually all control of their economy.

In 1989, the Albanian management and workers were summarily expelled from Trepća. The mineworkers' union organized a widely publicized march to Pristina in November, 1988, and in February, 1989, there was a hunger strike. Many miners and directors were arrested and imprisoned. Since then, the enterprise has been run exclusively by Belgrade in a very inefficient manner due to a lack of investment and poor maintenance. In February, 1995, Belgrade installed new management and a program of "revitalization" was undertaken. By the end of 1996 all the production plants were in operation, ore excavation had increased, and Trepća had exported $100 million worth of products, making it the largest exporting company in the FRY. In the meantime, the sacked Albanian miners were replaced first with Eastern European laborers and later with Bosnian prisoners of war and ethnic Serb refugees from Croatia and Bosnia.[8]

The Greek company Mytilineos Holding S.A. first entered the picture in December, 1995, when it started handling the marketing of minerals. In May, 1977, it signed a $517 million, five-year agreement that gave the company access to a hundred thousand tons of zinc and lead annually. In return, the Greek company would provide Trepća with working capital, financing, equipment, and additional quantities of ore. Six months later, Mytilineos Holding S.A. entered into a $1.2 billion, seven-year agreement with RTB-Bor in Serbia that gave the company access to a minimum of forty thousand tons of copper annually. In return, the Greek company would provide working capital financing, equipment, and spare parts and would participate in the financing of the modernization of the smelter. Serbia's RTB-Bor is Europe's second biggest copper producer outside of Russia.

It is crucial to understand that Trepća was not just any enterprise. As far as the Kosovo Albanians were concerned, the mines symbolized years of oppression and exploitation by the Serbs, as well as defiant acts of resistance. As Byrham Kavaja, an ethnic Albanian trade union leader said, "Trepća is something Albanians would give their lives for."[9]

Trepća was equally important to the Serbs—especially Milošević's regime, which relied on "crony corporatism." Under this system, state or "privatized" enterprises were run by the Serb leader's loyal friends—who in most cases also held government posts, thereby ensuring the *nomenklatura's* control over the economy and the jobs market. Trepća was the jewel in the crown of this system. According to Robert Fisk it was "Goodbye then to the monasteries and churches, the Serb Orthodox graves and mosaics and frescoes and Byzantine naves. Goodbye to the spiritual power of Kosovo. For here, deep within the mines of Trepća, lies the physical value of Slobodan Milošević's dangerous province, the wealthiest piece of real estate in the Balkans, the treasure house of Serbia valued—in proved and estimated reserves of land, zinc, cadmium, silver, and gold—at a mere £ 3 billion."[10]

Indeed, analysts like Chris Hedges have gone so far as to suggest that the war in Kosovo was to a large extent the result of Milošević's unwillingness to give up Trepća.[11] What, then, was so special about this Greek company that managed to gain an exclusive foothold in this most treasured part of Milošević's empire? What was the real nature of the deal? Who recommended the Greek company to Milošević?

When I interviewed Chairman Evangelos Mytilinaios in the summer of 1999, he claimed there was nothing special or sinister in the deals he entered into with the Serbs concerning Trepća and Bor. He told me he just landed one day in Belgrade and Milošević, duly impressed by his entrepreneurial acumen, decided to let him get involved in these two most precious and at the same time most sensitive enterprises.

"After the Dayton agreement," Mytilinaios said, "and as the result of the continuation of its isolation, Serbia was a country starved for cash. It was not at all difficult to go there and say: 'Give me the chance to make an investment and to exploit the wealth-producing resources of the country.' Western companies avoided going to Serbia either because they were prevented by their governments or because they were not getting export guarantees."[12]

Of course, not everybody saw the affair in such an innocent light. Articles appeared in the international press suggesting that the agreements the Greek company had signed were cover-ups for money-laundering schemes, and Mytilinaios was described as Slobodan Milošević's "money man." Finally, as the Kosovo Albanian newspaper *Koha Ditore* had written and as its editor Mr. Haxhi told me when I met him in Pristina in October of 1999, Mytilineos was very close to Mira Marković, Milošević's wife. Marković used to head the JUL Party, which was, in effect, a businessmen's party, and many of its members held important government posts. According to Tim Judah, JUL was "a useful arrangement for siphoning off public money."[13]

Mytilinaios flatly denied all these stories as unsubstantiated speculations: "If Mr. Milošević was a close friend of mine and if he had stayed in my yacht, I would say so just like [former Greek prime minister] Mitsotakis has done. But he is not." (Milošević occasionally spent his holidays in Greece with his good friend Constantine Mitsotakis and sailed around the Aegean islands on yachts belonging to prominent members of the Greek business elite.)

There are, however, some other interesting aspects of Mytilinaios's activities that must be considered. First, Mytilinaios also flirted with the banking business in Serbia, and at one time sought to acquire Slavia Bank, a small bank that has been inactive since losing its license for international operations but which still owns twenty-two branches. He was prepared to take a 20–25 percent stake in this bank. Secondly, he shared the copresidency of the Greek-Serb business council established in 1998 with Borca Vučić, who handled Milošević's personal finances. More importantly, it was her deft handling of various Serb offshore accounts while she was director of the Beogradska Bank branch in Cyprus during the war in Bosnia that prevented the total collapse of the FRY. Vučić was president of the Beogradska Bank, which owns Slavia Bank, until the change of regimes in Belgrade in October, 2000.

Finally, the reader should also bear in mind that the mineral industry is a prime candidate for money laundering. The variation in the quantity of ore concentrates, the varying degrees of extraction and processing costs, and price fluctuations in the final product make for the type of confusing opportunity for obfuscation that a money-laundering scheme needs. An example in point was the mid-1990 Hamanaća case in which the copper trade was allegedly used to conceal the illegal funds generated by the Southeast Asia drug trade.[14]

The issue that concerns us here, however, is not the behavior of a private Greek company. What concerns us is the policy of the Greek state. Consider some of the facts. In December, 1996, he was appointed to the board of directors of Greece's state-owned telecommunications company OTE. The appointment was certainly a surprise: Since when was a metal trader considered an expert in telecommunications? At the time the government claimed that the selection of a successful and dynamic young entrepreneur like Mytilinaios would greatly improve the image of the ailing state-owned company. Six months later—in June, 1997—another possible reason for the appointment emerged: OTE (in conjunction with Stet, the Italian telecommunications group) acquired 49 percent of Serbia Telecom for the bargain price of $1 billion. As *Financial Times* observed, this was Serbia's "biggest foreign investment deal 'and at the same time marked OTE's first strategic alliance outside Greece and reflects the close economic ties between Greece and Serbia.'"[15]

Yet from Belgrade's point of view, the deal had less to do with economics than with politics. With presidential and parliamentary elections looming later that year, the deal provided Serbian president Milošević's Socialist Party with the much-needed cash to meet several months' unpaid wages owed to public sector workers. "The deal," the *Economist* observed, "has propped up the regime of Slobodan Milošević."[16] Saša Mirković, vice president of independent Belgrade radio station B92, made the same point: "OTE in effect financed Milošević's electoral victory in 1997. It bought a big chunk of Serbia Telecom at a ridiculously low price but in cash. This cash disappeared in no time!"[17] Moreover, it is interesting to note that Mytilinaios's purchase of Slavia Bank was to have been financed in part by the state-owned National Bank of Greece.

Another area where the interests of the Greek businessman, the Greek state, and Serbia met was in the lucrative field of arms procurement. Through its subsidiary Metka, Mytilineos Holding was able to secure some large defense contracts to produce submarines and Patriot missiles for the Greek military. At the same time, Metka was also involved with the state-owned Yugoslav power company. In effect, Metka had undertaken the construction of infrastructure work and the modernization of the Yugoslav public utility.[18]

Moreover, and this is a central point, Mytilineos's economic activities in Kosovo took place with the knowledge and encouragement of various Greek governments over the protests of the Kosovo Albanians. President-elect Ibrahim Rugova repeatedly warned foreign investors throughout the 1990s that any deal they made with the Serbs concerning the exploitation of Kosovo's resources should also have his approval. Otherwise, the deals would be considered "null and void."

When Rugova learned about the deal between Mytilineos Holding and Belgrade, he asked the Greek company not to go ahead with the plan without the approval of the "Albanian authorities in Kosovo." At the same time, he asked Greek authorities not to condone the deal because "such actions add more difficulties to the already difficult situation in Kosovo and hurt our good relations with Greece."

In May, 1997, the Albanian board managing Trepća denounced the deal between Mytilineos Holding and the Serb government. According to the newspaper *Bujku* published in Pristina, the legitimate Trepća management and the people who had been fired by the Serbian regime called on the Greek government to ensure that the contract was annulled, while at the same time pointing out that failure to do so would contribute to a further increase in the political tensions and aggravation of the economic situation in Kosovo.[19]

When asked why he had disregarded Rugova's warning, Mytilinaios responded: "I am a businessman. The political issue of the decision I leave to the politicians. In this case when I heard the reaction of Ibrahim Rugova I immediately contacted the Greek Foreign Office and asked their opinion. I stressed to them that I did not want to come into conflict with the Albanians since this was a political issue. They replied: "Do not worry about Rugova. We will deal with him. You just go ahead with the deal. "And when they said 'go ahead' it was not just words: They proceeded to grant me export guarantees. When the state gives you export guarantees knowing fully well what you are up to, that means that they support you. That was the position of the Greek government. What was I supposed to do?"[20]

This incident was indicative of the fact that all the deals the Greek Company made with Milošević's regime were done with the explicit approval if not guidance of the Greek government. At the same time, this incident also showed the contempt with which the Greek State treated the Albanian Kosovars and their leaders.

Sadly, it was not only the Greek government that disregarded the wishes of the Kosovo Albanians. The same attitude was also exhibited by institutions like the trade unions, which in the West are conceptualized as being parts of "civil society" (a term that makes little if any sense in societies dominated by ethno national ideologies)

The Albanian miners in Kosovo issued an appeal through the Durham Chapter of the British National Union of Miners (NUM) asking for the support of their Greek colleagues. "We have heard," stated the letter sent by the Durham NUM chapter to the Greek trade unions, "that a Greek company, Mytilineos S.A., has signed a deal with the Trepća mining company in Kosovo whereby Mytilineos will invest 500 million dollars to extract minerals from Kosovo. This deal has been done without any consultation with the Kosovo Miners, who are legally still the owners of the mines. No proposal has been made to employ them at the mines. The United Independent Trade Unions of Kosovo have asked us to help them in this matter. We are therefore appealing to our fellow trade unionists in Greece to help our brother miners in Kosovo."

Nothing happened. The Greek trade unions claimed they never received the appeal and that they were unaware of the history of the Trepća miners. In any event, at the time they were as busy protesting NATO's efforts to save the Bosnians from annihilation as they had been a few years earlier organizing mass receptions for Orthodox war hero Radovan Karadžić. The appeal of the Kosovo and British miners fell on deaf ears. The days of international worker solidarity were definitely over. Worker solidarity had given way to ethnic solidarity; the red flag had been replaced by the Byzantine Orthodox double-headed eagle and cross. No longer did miners singing the "International" lead the demonstrations. Instead, dark-clad priests and voter-hungry politicians chanted religious hymns mourning the fall of Constantinople.

The final days of the Milošević regime in October, 2000, were greeted throughout the free world with feelings of relief if not euphoria. But there was one exception. There was one country in Europe where the events unfolding in Serbia did not seem to cause any feelings of joy. That country was Greece. It would not be an overstatement to say that the overwhelming majority of the political forces and people of that country reacted to the events in Serbia with feelings of disenchantment if not dismay. To the very end, members of the Greek government and of the opposition went out of their way to please Milošević in their official statements.

The fact that Greece was certainly not going to side with the Serbian opposition was made patently clear a couple of weeks prior to the elections. The Serb student opposition group OTPOR had the idea of organizing a public concert in Salonika. "We believe," said Slobodan Honem, a leading OTPOR activist, "that a massively attended anti-Milošević concert in Greece would send a strong message to the people of Serbia. Namely that it is not only the Western powers that want Milošević's ouster but also the people of a friendly country like Greece." However, what the OTPOR activists failed to understand was that, as I have argued in the previous pages, Greece's sympathies lay not so much with Serbia in general as with the Milošević regime and its henchmen in Bosnia and Kosovo. Needless to say, none of the major Greek music groups or artists that had distinguished themselves in anti-NATO events during the wars in Kosovo and Bosnia agreed to take part in the anti-Milošević concert. Moreover, the few minor music groups that did were subjected to all forms of threats and harassment aimed at discouraging their participation.

The concert was supposed to take place in a state-owned concert hall that fell under the jurisdiction of the prefect of Salonika. Two days before the event was scheduled to take place, the prefect, Kostas Papadopoulos, a prominent member of the governing PASOK Party, decided to cancel it because, he argued, it would interfere in the politics of another country.[21]

This probably marked the first time in recent Greek history that the authorities tried to prevent a political gathering. Countless public events linked to international politics have been permitted, celebrating the likes of Palestinian Abu Nidal, the Kurd Abdullah Ocalan, Saddam Hussein, and, more recently, indicted Bosnian Serb war criminal Radovan Karadzic. Yet no one ever expressed a desire to ban them. Even more significant was the fact that neither of the two major parties that represent 90 percent of the electorate protested the prefect's action.

Trying to prevent an anti-Milošević event in Greece was a sign of things to come. Both during and after the September elections in Yugoslavia, Greek authorities spared no effort in trying to legitimize the electoral results and generally in supporting the ousted dictator. The first such attempt was made by the "independent" monitors Slobodan Milošević invited from Greece. They included Alexandros Lykourezos, a member of the ND Party who at the same time was also Ratko Mladić's lawyer; Liana Kaneli, a communist deputy who, according to press reports, was being chauffeured around in Milošević's limo during the war in Kosovo; and Aris Mousionis, president of the Greek-Serb Friendship Association. The monitoring committee was led by Karolos Papoulias, a former Greek foreign minister and at the time chairman of the foreign affairs committee of the Greek Parliament.

Upon returning from Belgrade, Papoulias stated that the election process in Yugoslavia had taken place smoothly and democratically.[22] This assessment of the situation was immediately adopted by the Greek government and became its official mantra. Government spokesman Dimitris Repas stated that the elections had gone smoothly and that there was no reason to question the outcome.[23] The next day he reiterated this view, adding that the end result would be fair to all.[24]

If anybody had expected the Yugoslav elections to provide an opportunity for Kostas Simitis's government to change its policies and improve Greece's image, which had been tarnished by its association with the Belgrade regime, this was a great disappointment. Greece once again had differentiated its policies from those of the Western democracies and of the Serb opposition.

Both the West and the Serb opposition had immediately pointed out the grave irregularities in the election. Indeed, the only country that seemed to share the Greek government's uncritical acceptance of the fairness of the election was Iraq. "The election," said Iraq's internal affairs minister, Muhammed Zaman Abdel Razak, echoing the Greek view, "took place freely and without any pressures being exercised."[25] Russian ultranationalist Vladimir Zhirinovsky voiced a similar opinion.

In Belgrade and the rest of Yugoslavia, the opposition was busy denouncing the electoral fraud and organizing massive strikes and demonstrations aimed at toppling Milošević and preventing him from holding a second round of elections. While the Serb people took to the streets by the hundred of thousands, the Greek government rushed to help the Serb oligarch by supporting his demands for holding a new election.

In an interview with the Greek radio station "Flash," Foreign Minister George Papandreou advised the Serb opposition to yield to Milošević's pressure and take part in the election. "Our advice, coming from our own experience," he said, "is that abstention even under very harsh conditions, even under conditions which are not fully democratically controlled, is not the best solution."[26]

Minister of Defense Akis Tsochatzopoulos was less subtle: "The election results pointed toward the path leading to a second round."[27] Until the very last moment, the Greek government continued trying to convince the Serb opposition to participate in a second election.[28]

The Serb opposition adamantly rejected the Greek proposal. N. Bakarec, an adviser to Vojislav Koštunica, speaking on behalf of his candidate, said: "Greece is a friendly country but its intervention in our internal affairs bears no relation to reality. We cannot accept a second round [of elections] irrespective of what we get in return."[29] Had the opposition followed Greece's advice, Milošević would still be in power today.

It must be stressed at this point that the Greek government's pro-Milošević attitude was shared by the majority of Greek political forces as well as by the majority of the people. Indicative of the attitude of the ND Party were statements made by its honorary leader, former prime minister Constantine Mitsotakis. "The policy of NATO and the U.S.—which openly and provocatively intervened in the elections even as they followed an inexplicable policy toward Kosovo and Montenegro—essentially harmed the opposition," he said. He called for the "immediate lifting of the embargo" and "the abandonment of a policy of one-sided prosecution of war criminals." Mitsotakis also called on the Simitis goverment to distance itself from the West: "The role of Greece cannot be that of a rearguard in a wrong-headed policy, which is rejected by the overwhelming majority of the Greek people and which can have negative repercussions in the country."[30]

Mitsotakis was right in at least one thing: his assessment of the support that Slobodan Milošević enjoyed among the overwhelming majority of the Greek population. According to a poll taken in Greece by the Athens radio station "Flash" during the huge Thursday afternoon demonstration that led to the toppling of Milošević's regime, 65 percent of respondents said that his fall was a sinister plot engineered by the West and the United States. Only 30 percent of those queried hailed the event as a victory for democracy and popular sovereignty.

The Milošević-Greece drama entered its highest and perhaps final stage on June 26, 2001, the day the Serb leader was extradited to The Hague to appear before the International Crimes Tribunal. When the news reached Athens that Milošević's extradition was imminent, a process of signature collection among the Greek deputies was set in motion. Within a few hours, seventy-nine deputies representing all of Greece's political parties had signed a petition asking the Serb government not to hand over the former leader. No more than a hundred deputies were thought to be in Athens taking part in Parliament's summer session at the time.

What was most noteworthy about the statement was not that it questioned the tribunal's impartiality, but that it included a demand that no Serb war criminal be handed over to the UN established court. It was the first time such a far-reaching demand was formulated in such an explicit manner by a group of deputies representing the overwhelming majority of Greece's political forces. Equally noteworthy was the fact that no Greek political party denounced this act.[31]

The Greek Foreign Office issued a statement that diverged sharply both in form as well as substance from corresponding statements by its NATO partners. As far as the form was concerned, the triumphalist tone that characterized the Western governments' statements was notably absent from the Greek communiqué. The latter simply stated that the question of Milošević's extradition was a Yugoslavian internal matter to be decided solely by the government and political forces of the country.[32] The substance also differed. By stating that the question of Milošević's extradition was "solely" a matter for the Yugoslav government to decide, the Greek communiqué in effect questioned the primacy of international law even in cases involving such serious offences as crimes against humanity and war crimes—the very charges for which Slobodan Milošević was indicted.

The night of the extradition, a spontaneous demonstration by nearly four thousand Milošević supporters took place in downtown Athens. A corresponding demonstration in Belgrade at the same time drew no more than a thousand participants.

As we saw earlier, Slobodan Milošević proposed in December, 1994, that Greece and Serbia form a confederation.[33] Andreas Papandreou, who at the time was serving as Greek prime minister, called the proposal "interesting," but the matter was put to rest. Surely Milošević feels sorry that he did not pursue the matter further. Had his plan for a Greek-Serb federation materialized, he might well have won the 2000 election. The majority of Greeks would have voted for him at any rate.

Ideology
and Institutions

CHAPTER 7

The Radicalization of the Orthodox Church

The attitudes that shaped the reactions of Greek society to the events in Kosovo and Bosnia cannot be understood if one fails to take into account the developments in one of the major institutional strongholds of anti-Western ideology: namely, the Orthodox Church of Greece. While the politicization of religion in Turkey has commanded considerable attention internationally, little attention has been paid to corresponding developments in the Orthodox Church. Yet the politicization of the Greek Orthodox Church may be considered one of the most important recent developments in the country.

There is, of course, tremendous variance in the way this process takes place in different countries. One of the main differences pertains to the goals of the respective religious movements. While in Turkey Muslims mainly seek to reform the domestic agenda, in Greece the church has increasingly focused on issues pertaining to the country's foreign policy. Moreover, its statements usually express strong nationalist viewpoints.

In 1992 the Greek Church was in the vanguard of opposition to the neighboring state's plan to call itself Macedonia.[1] It played a decisive role in fermenting nationalist feelings by organizing and participating in the mass rallies protesting the "usurpation" of the name Macedonia held all over Greece during the 1990s. The mass demonstrations in Salonika and Athens in which the church played a major role showed that it was in a position to create political events that would have a decisive influence on the formation of Greece's foreign policy. The aim of the demonstrations was to put pressure on the Greek government to show intransigence and to refuse any compromise

12. A Greek priest leads a demonstration in Athens to confirm the nonseparation of church and state in Greece. Photo courtesy Eleftherotypia.

on the Macedonia issue. This was asserted by Bishop Panteleimon of Salonika during a mass attended by the president of Greece and other state dignitaries: "The nation will hold you responsible for the name Macedonia, which for us is not up for bargaining."[2] The Greek Orthodox Church stuck to this attitude throughout the 1990s. As recently as March, 2001, Archbishop Christodoulos reiterated the church's opposition to the name Macedonia by quoting those who feared it would eventually legitimize the young country's claims to Greek territory.[3]

Moreover, high-ranking church dignitaries were openly involved in actions that may have led to the destabilization of the Albanian state by providing at least spiritual support to movements that sought the union of Northern Epirus (southern Albania), where a Greek minority resides, with Greece. In May, 1994, Bishop Sevastianos of Konitsa in northern Greece asked that Greek tanks be sent to Northern Epirus. A few weeks later—in a speech delivered on June 2 to Greek foreign minister Karolos Papoulias, representatives from other political parties, and thousands of cheering, flag-waving supporters of Bishop Panteleimon—Sevastianos called for the region's annexation by Greece.[4]

Similar support occasionally was expressed in statements that challenged both the law of the land and international conventions. A case in point concerned an attack on the guardhouse at Episkopi, which lay on the Albanian side of the border, by the Greek paramilitary organization MAVI in October, 1994. The attack resulted in the death of two Albanian guards and the wounding of two others. Several MAVI activists were arrested on March 19, 1995, brought to trial, and eventually set free because of a lack of evidence. An editorial in a bimonthly journal published by the Diocese of Dimitrias called the Greek paramilitary group's act "patriotic and heroic." The national interest, the paper argued, should take precedence over the demands of justice. "Even if they are guilty, their deeds should be covered up. Who will dare to undertake a similar risky mission in the future knowing that the government will not help him conceal it?"[5]

Although the Greek Church played an active role in promoting pro-Serb feelings in Greece while at the same time fueling anti-Western and anti-American sentiment with its militant rhetoric, its pronouncements on foreign policy issues have not been restricted to events related to the recent Balkans wars. Since his election to the church's top office in May, 1998, Archbishop Christodoulos has devoted considerable attention to foreign policy and implicitly calls for the "liberation" of "unredeemed" areas in that country where Greek minorities have resided.

Archbishop Christodoulos's strong nationalist views did not suddenly appear with his assumption of the church's top leadership position. During a conflict over an islet in the Aegean Sea that brought Greece and Turkey close to war in the winter of 1996, he wrote an article for *To Vima* denouncing the peaceful outcome of the crisis and advocating a military solution to the problem: "The choice we are confronted with is peace or freedom, peace or national humiliation. And when confronted with this dilemma the correct historical choice cannot be peace."[6]

Yet since his election, Archbishop Christodoulos's anti-Turkish pronouncements have gathered new force. Not only has he been prone to denounce the "barbaric east" (i.e., Turkey) whenever the occasion presents itself, but he also has sought to rekindle Greek irredentism dreams with talk of "returning" to the "unredeemed homelands" *(alitrotes patrides)* of northeastern Turkey, which once held a sizable Greek population. Another noteworthy foreign policy statement came at the end of August, 1998, when, in the company of other church dignitaries, he called for the "recapture" of Constantinople and Hagia Sofia from Turkey.[7] The leader of the Greek Church has also formulated policy positions in relation to the Cyprus problem. Cyprus has been divided since 1974, after the Turkish army invaded the island in response to a Greek-inspired military coup against President Makarios. The Greek archbishop has rejected the UN-sponsored framework of intercommunal talks, which center on the idea of a bizonal federal state.[8]

The views and foreign policy agenda of the Greek Orthodox Church are of tremendous importance if one takes into consideration the symbiotic nature of state-church relations in Greece. The church has considerable institutional power—derived partly from the country's constitution, which establishes the inseparability of church and state in Greece, and partly from the church's purported historical connection with the Greek nation, which the church supposedly "saved " from extinction during Ottoman rule.

The Greek Orthodox Church also enjoys considerable privileges in relation to other churches and religions—a fact that is seen by many as imposing severe restraints on the principle of religious freedom and as discriminating against various religious minorities.[9]

The nonseparation of church and state in Greece endows the Greek Church with political significance while at the same time ensuring the acceptance of its views by a wide section of the public.[10] Nevertheless, Kostas Simitis's PASOK government, like those before it, has stated that it does not intend to tamper with the principle of nonseparation. In a recent official statement, George Paschalidis, minister of Macedonia and Thrace, reaffirmed that the Greek government opposes the separation of church and state.[11]

Even such earlier paragons of political radicalism as the late Andreas Papandreou did not miss an opportunity to show their devotion to the Orthodox creed. Throughout the 1990s Papandreou toured monasteries around the country while his new wife, ex-stewardess Dimitra Liani, would declare her unwavering commitment to the church's teachings whenever the occasion presented itself.[12]

However one sees the Greek Orthodox Church, despite occasional disagreements with the government,[13] it remains, in Paschalis Kitromilides's phrase, the "official arm of the civil state." This applies especially to the realm of foreign policy. The church's positions in relation to Macedonia and the war in Yugoslavia, although expressed in a language not free from hyperbole, in essence reflected the views held at the time by the overwhelming majority of the Greek political class. It can thus be argued that the foreign policy function of the Orthodox Greek Church today is to help the Greek state maximize its influence in neighboring countries whose people share the same religion.

This newfound—after the fall of communism—political importance of the Orthodox Church in the Balkans was immediately sensed by Prime Minister Papandreou, who accorded to religion a crucial place in shaping Greek foreign policy. In 1994 he stated that the Balkan wars had "brought to the surface the resonance of Orthodox ties" between Athens, Sofia, Belgrade, Bucharest, and Moscow, and reconfirmed the Orthodox bond uniting the people of some Balkan countries.[14] Two years earlier, during one of his speeches to Socialist Party militants, Papandreou had stressed that the ties uniting Greece and Serbia were grounded on the fact that the two nations had fought together in the Balkan wars as well as on the fact that they shared a common religion.[15]

What is noteworthy about those statements is not so much their novelty as the fact that they came from a leftist politician. As for the novelty of the views linking foreign policy with religion, Andreas Papandreou was simply following in the footsteps of Antonis Samaras, who as foreign minister was the first prominent politician to articulate a strategic vision of Greek national interests involving the creation of alliances based on religious ties (the famous Orthodox arc or axis).[16]

The fact that the church had an institutional role to play in the articulation of Greece's foreign policy was once again underlined at a meeting held in 1998 between Foreign Minister Theodoros Pangalos and Archbishop

Christodoulos. The purpose of the meeting was to explore ways in which the Greek Church could contribute to Greece's Balkan foreign policy agenda. According to the archbishop, "We explored ways to promote the interests of our nation and to make good use of the relations we have with the Balkan Churches in the North who follow the same faith as we do." He also expressed his "wish for a close and good cooperation between the Church and the Foreign Office." In his reply, Pangalos was only too eager to express his agreement with this "national" role of the church: "The Ministry of Foreign Affairs believes that the Church of Greece has a major mission to play in the Orthodox world as well as elsewhere."[17]

What was this mission? It was nothing less than the creation of an alliance—an "arc" as it was called—of Orthodox countries in the Balkans. This vision was outlined in an article Christodoulos wrote in 1993 while serving as bishop of the Diocese of Dimitrias. In it, he called upon Serbs, Russians, Romanians, Greeks, and Bulgarians to lay aside their petty differences and unite in the formation of an alliance that would become the vanguard of the Christian West's fight against the Muslims. Naturally, he expected the Greek Orthodox Church to play a "decisive" role in forming this alliance.[18]

The nationalist positions advocated by the Greek Orthodox Church reflect not so much the metaphysics of Orthodoxy as the church's role as an institution of the Greek state. From its emergence at the close of the nineteenth century to the present day, the Greek state has used the Orthodox Church as one of its main instruments for achieving ethnic homogeneity in the territories under its control—especially in northern Greece. In that sense, the function of the Greek Church in what Sabrina Ramet calls the promotion of national mythologies and collective loyalty has been paramount.[19] The nationalization of the church, according to Kitromilides, proved an "irreversible process" that culminated in "the total conversion of the Church of Greece to the secular values of Greek nationalism to the point that the Church of Greece spearheaded all nationalist initiatives in the latter part of the nineteenth and throughout the twentieth centuries: from the promotion of the irredentist ideology of the Megali Idea in the early twentieth century to its participation in the rallies and demonstrations against the Republic of Macedonia, against NATO and for the Serbs."[20]

Russian theologian Alexander Schmemann uses the term "theological nationalism" to describe the nationalism that dominates the Greek Orthodox Church. According to Schmemann, the more general attempt by the Greeks to appropriate the whole of Orthodoxy in the Greek religious worldview is both "anti-historical" as well as "a-historical." This attempt, he argues, contains a double mythology that is partly religious and partly secular. On one hand the Greeks sought to nationalize the Byzantine and the Orthodox tradition and on the other to achieve the secularization of the Orthodox religion by its identification not only with the Greek state but also with classical Greece. The latter, representing "paganism," was until the very end the great enemy of theocratic Byzantium and of the Orthodox Church.[21]

The secularization of society in the West has altered the role of Christian churches. Religion no longer serves as society's principal reference point. It has been replaced by nationalism. In Greece, as well as in other nations that emerged from the dissolution of the Ottoman Empire, the process took a different route. Here, the Orthodox Church has become an essential component of nationalist ideology. "The construction of national identities among the Orthodox Christians in the dismembered Empires," argues Adamantia Pollis, "invariably reincorporated religion as a crucial component of the newly constructed nationality. The ethnos (nation) and Orthodoxy became a unity. To be Greek necessitates being Greek Orthodox just as to be Russian necessitates being a Russian Orthodox."[22] It is indicative of the total identification of the Greek Church with the nation that, as Victoria Clark points out, even foreign converts to the Greek Church eventually end

13. *Hundreds of thousands participated in a rally organized in Athens by the Greek Church in the spring of 2000. The aim of the demonstration was to confirm the belief that "Greece means Orthodoxy." Photo courtesy* Eleftherotypia.

up adopting not only the theological dogmas of the Orthodox creed but also the foreign policy positions of the Greek government.[23]

The Orthodox religion today constitutes one of the decisive semantic "markers" of modern Greek ethnic identity. The leader of the Greek Church constantly stresses the nation's identification with Orthodoxy. The most recent restatement of this position happened at an Athens rally attended by hundreds of thousands of people. There, Archbishop Christodoulos reiterated that "Greece means Orthodoxy."[24] At a luncheon for foreign correspondents held a few days before the rally he said, "Orthodoxy defines the identity of every Greek."[25]

The nationalization of religion in Greece as expressed in the conjunction of the ethnos and religion was also made manifest in the church leader's statements conflating national interests with the interests of the Orthodox religion. For example, when replying to critics who had asked him to refrain from making statements on foreign policy issues, Christodoulos said: "I will not stop expressing the interests of the Nation. And I believe that my mission is to support the national interest whatever the costs."[26]

Antonis Manitakis, professor of constitutional law at the University of Salonika, recently observed: "The Archbishop said that he is interested in matters that concern the nation and not as one would have expected in matters that concern the poor, the unemployed, the marginalized, the refugees. The guidelines he follows in his speeches are not those of the Gospel or

14. Archbishop Christodoulos of the Greek Orthodox Church addresses a mass rally in Athens in the spring of 2000. Photo courtesy Eleftherotypia.

15. *A Greek priest holds the country's flag during a rally in Athens in the spring of 2000. Photo courtesy* Eleftherotypia.

the Word of the Lord, but of the national interest. This seems to be for him the supreme value."[27]

This identification of the archbishop with the "interests of the nation" means that, despite Greek Orthodoxy's claims to universality, its real mission is "to preserve the superior spiritual ethos of Greekness by forging a symbiotic relationship between Church and state, a task simplified by the fact that the overwhelming majority of Greeks are Orthodox. The Church's self-proclaimed duty to preserve this transcendent ethnos (along with the financial privileges for itself and its clergy) has strengthened a long-standing Church-state interdependence."[28]

The interaction of the state with the church in Greece in recent years seems to parallel similar developments in the state-church relationship in Serbia.[29] In both cases, the state and the established church have promoted the notion that the national identity is coextensive with Orthodoxy. But they have done so for different reasons. From the point of view of the state, this symbiotic relationship has helped create a myth of cultural unity that in turn has provided the main legitimacy for nationalist aspirations. But the established church also derives benefits from this state of affairs. Not only does the Orthodox Church of Greece enjoy extensive privileges in relation to other religions, it has also been placed at the ideological center and its discourse has been endowed with political significance and public relevance.

The discourse of the Greek Church will acquire more prominence in the years to come. As the traditional political elites increasingly find themselves unable—either because of the country's international obligations or because of the system of cosmopolitan values their members are made to espouse— to articulate effectively the fundamental anti-Western worldview inherent in the ethnocultural ideology of modern Greece, the church will be asked to fill the vacuum. The great irony may well turn out to be that the salvation of ethnic nationalism in Greece and perhaps elsewhere will increasingly come to depend on the Orthodox Church. The social forces that will bear the church's ideology are already in place. As Helena Smith, the British newspaper *Guardian*'s correspondent in Greece, observed, Christodoulos draws his support from the marginalized petit-bourgeoisie, unskilled workers, disgruntled civil servants, and the small-time self-employed. For them, "The Church is the only bulwark left against the threat of a multicultural open society symbolised . . . by the yuppies who work for multinationals, drive jeeps and wield mobiles like firearms."[30]

That these are not idle speculations is shown by two polls. The most recent, conducted in December, 2000, by the Greek National Center of

Social Research (EKKE), showed that secondary school students, parents, and teachers, ranked the church as the most trustworthy of various institutions in Greek society. The army came second, and Parliament was relegated to a very low place.[31] In the other poll, conducted in 1998, 76.4 percent of respondents said that they preferred Archbishop Christodoulos, Greece's most militant nationalist and anti-Western leader, over Prime Minister Kostas Simitis and opposition leader Kostas Karamanlis, who represent the modernizing and cosmopolitan political elite.[32]

CHAPTER 8

The Logic of Ethnic Nationalism

T he blind solidarity which Greeks feel toward the Serbs is totally incomprehensible," asserted French philosopher Alain Finkielkraut in 1994. "In my eyes, Greece has ceased being a part of Europe, it has become de-Europeanized."[1]

Yet what, precisely, was "incomprehensible" in the Greek reactions to what was happening in Croatia, Bosnia, and Kosovo? And in what sense was Greece becoming "de-Europeanized"? It was certainly not incomprehensible to oppose the hasty dissolution of Yugoslavia or the exclusive demonization of the Serbs, as was perhaps the habit in many areas around the world. Nor was it incomprehensible to believe that bombing Serbia would not necessarily solve the Kosovo problem. Finally, it was by no means incomprehensible to oppose the embargo imposed on Serbia by the international community. One could disagree with those views that were dominant in Greece, but they were rational views that could be supported with recourse to rational argumentation and discussion. Moreover, they were by no means restricted to the Greeks.

What was incomprehensible, however, was the fact that Greek society did not seem to be affected by the feelings of horror that other nations in the West experienced upon learning about the atrocities being committed by the Serbs and Bosnian Serbs in Bosnia and Kosovo. It was not so much the case that Greeks were not sufficiently informed—although that was also a part of the story—but that they did not *want* to be informed: They preferred to consciously close their eyes and ears to all evidence of Serb atrocities. Moreover, when it became impossible to continue claiming ignorance, the overwhelming majority of Greeks failed to exhibit the moral revulsion one would expect. In this respect, Finkielkraut was right: Greece's stance was indeed "incomprehensible."

Let us consider some facts. During the war in Kosovo a poll was taken to test the Greek public's reaction to events.[2] The poll revealed that 96 percent of Greeks opposed NATO air strikes against Serbia and 94 percent were dissatisfied with the European Union's handling of the problem. Those results were not surprising given the general climate of opinion that prevailed in the country. They seemed to simply confirm what everybody knew: namely that the majority of Greeks passionately opposed the air strikes against Serbia. The poll did, however, contain one interesting surprise: When asked to evaluate various political leaders, 64 percent of respondents said they had a good opinion of Slobodan Milošević. On the other hand, the elected leaders of liberal democratic countries fared rather poorly: Only 5 percent thought positively of Tony Blair, and Bill Clinton favorably impressed only 4 percent of respondents.

The results of the poll were truly revealing: They showed for the first time that the Greek opposition to NATO bombings did not simply express a lack of support for military action, as the Greek government had been fond of arguing. The poll showed that the Greek public's opposition to NATO military action was related to an affinity the majority of Greeks felt for Belgrade, its leader, and his ethnotribal policies.

This was further confirmed by the fact that 53 percent of respondents believed Milošević and his government had violated Albanians' human rights in Kosovo. In other words, Greeks were aware that atrocities were taking place, and that fact did not influence their evaluation of Slobodan Milošević. This element, which is essential in deconstructing Greek reactions, cannot be explained as simply a by-product of Greece's culturally and historically conditioned pro-Serbian feelings. The absence of feelings of moral outrage to the violations of human rights in Bosnia first and Kosovo later derived from the structural imperatives that define the ideological content of modern Greece's national identity. The tolerance that Greek society exhibited toward the crimes being committed in Bosnia and Kosovo can thus be seen as resulting from the structural constraints of a particular type of society: namely a society dominated by the ideology of ethnic (as opposed to civic) nationalism. The lack of human rights concerns in the evaluation of the unfolding drama in the former Yugoslavia followed from the very nature of the ideology of ethnonationalism that to a large extent defines modern Greece's identity and ideology.

As noted in the introduction to this book, the main difference between ethnic and civic nationalism is that in the former the legitimacy of a nation state is rooted in exclusive ethnicity whereas in the latter it is rooted in the civic nationalism of citizenship. In the former, the collective nature of society, which is composed of members who share a cultural identity, is stressed. In the latter, a "nation" is simply a body of citizens, and only their political rights—not their cultural identities—matter.[3] This division also has profound implications for the conceptualization and implementation of human rights in the respective states.[4]

Citizenship, to the extent that it symbolizes a commitment to particular institutions, contains within it the potentiality of respecting the rights of groups of people who do not share the ethnic characteristics of the numerically dominant group. By contrast, in ethnonational states, the emphasis on exclusivity seriously impairs the recognition of the rights of members of "other" groups. In ethnonational states, the moral space is defined on the axis of "authenticity." A distinction persists between nationals and citizens: Those who are not of the proper ethnicity, even if they are citizens, are considered to be "others" and thus not viewed as "authentic" nationals. Ethnonational states construct an identity anchored on the indispensable ethnic features of an authentic member of a nation. These are the "markers" that define the substance of each particular ethnic group and proclaim its uniqueness and distinctiveness vis-à-vis other ethnic groups.

Modern Greece, as we have seen, is an ethnonational state par excellence. The primary distinctive features or markers of modern Greek ethnicity are mainly language and religion. These are attributes of all "authentic" Greeks. The absence of either of these markers singles people out as "others" even if their ancestors resided in the region for centuries.[5] Moreover, these "others" are viewed as a source of potential danger to social cohesion and/or Greece's national sovereignty and territorial integrity. A report released in the winter of 2001 by the European Monitoring Center on Racism and Xenophobia (EUMC) seemed once again to confirm the pervasiveness of the fears that still exist in Greece concerning the presence of cultural "others." This report contains the results of a Eurobarometer survey of citizens of nations in the European Union who were asked to consider whether it is a good thing for any society to be made up of people from different races, religions, and cultures. While 64 percent of European Union citizens agreed that this was a good thing, in Greece the corresponding percentage was a mere 36. In fact, Greece was at the bottom of the Eurobarometer ranking of all EU countries with regard to their tolerance of the existence of "others" in their midst.[6]

Greek reactions to the mayhem in neighboring Yugoslavia were conditioned by moral precepts that have their origin in the logic of the building
of Balkan ethnonational states. Greece, like the other countries in the region, saw itself as building "a new state amid basically unfriendly populations" after the annexation of the "New Lands" following the Balkan wars.[7]
The fact that Greeks did not feel any revulsion about the crimes being committed in Bosnia could be said to reflect the inability of the people of a state
based on ethnic exclusivity to consider as a crime something that they, in
many respects, viewed as natural. In ethnonational states, violating the rights
of a person who does not share the ethnic markers of a group is not considered a crime on a par with violating the rights of a person belonging to the
same group. People living in ethnonational states have rights mainly to the
extent that they are bearers of particular ethnic markers and not because
they are members of an abstract humanity. Rights are "ethnic," not "human." As Peter Sugar argues, Eastern nationalism "claims rights for a chosen
people, not the individual or citizen."[8]

In the context of the worldview of ethnonationalism, the ethnic cleansing of "others" is viewed as a normal step on the road to ethnic homogenization. According to Anthony Smith, ethnic purification is part of the logic of
ethnic nationalism even when people do *not* act out its precepts.[9] The mass
extermination of "others" is considered a regrettable, but in certain cases
unavoidable, aspect of policies aimed at forging ethnically pure states. Exchange of populations is again seen as unavoidable since the presence of
"others" would pollute the purity of the ethnic nation and leave it vulnerable to its enemies. It is interesting, as Nikiforos Diamantouros of Athens
University notes, that in Greece the population exchanges between Greece
and Turkey that took place in the early 1920s are morally condemned not
because they constitute by-products of ethnic nationalism, but because they
signify the loss of "unredeemed Greek homelands" due to foreign "dark conspiracies."[10]

Serb demands to carve up Bosnia into ethnically pure areas were met in
Greece with understanding since, according to the logic of the ethnonational
state, the welfare of a particular ethnic group cannot be guaranteed in a
political community threatened by the presence of "others."

Historically conditioned sympathy for the Serbs and dislike of Croatians
and Muslims was, of course, an important factor in Greece's reaction. After
all, the Greek state shares an important ethnic marker (i.e., the Orthodox
Christian religion) with the Serbs that it does not share with the "others"
(Croats, Bosnians). Moreover, during the wars in the former Yugoslavia

another myth gained prominence in Greece. According to this myth, the Serbs had "traditionally" and "always" been Greece's friends and allies. But these factors were secondary in accounting for the Greek reactions to the mayhem in Bosnia and Kosovo.

The conceptual scheme that underlined the responses of the Greek state and society resulted primarily from the imperatives that define the moral space of ethnonational states. Ultimately, the understanding the Greek political elites and the people showed for the practices of "ethnic cleansing" in Bosnia resulted from the fact that the logic underpinning and influencing the state-building strategies in Greece have been ethnic. The ethnicity of the dominant national group served as the organizing as well as exclusive principle informing its nationalism—with serious consequences for the cultural "others."

"The non-recognition of other ethnic groups, which such an arrangement implies, narrowed the social foundation upon which the nationalist ideology rested . . . and often gave rise to strategies of coping with the problem, which adhered to one of the three alternative logics, assimilation, expulsion, or liquidation."[11]

The opposition between Greece and the West over Bosnia and Kosovo thus did not stem from different strategic evaluations of a similar situation, nor from different historically conditioned sympathies. It stemmed from the incompatibility of two radically different conceptual paradigms: Balkan ethnonationalism on one hand versus European civic nationalism on the other.

"The self-determination of the Balkan areas," writes French historian François Thual, "does not tolerate the presence of ethnic or religious minorities: Turks in Greece or Hungarians in Rumania. Thus, in order to reach the fulfillment of their ethnicity . . . the minorities must be gotten rid of or assimilated or condemned to silence. According to this logic, the 'Other' cannot coexist in the same space. He constitutes an obstacle, and his continued existence signifies a possible threat."[12]

That is the reason why the majority of Greeks could combine awareness of Slobodan Milošević's human rights violations with a deep respect and admiration for his person and his policies. If Milošević was violating the human rights of the "others" that was only "natural"—albeit perhaps regrettable when it was being overdone—and should certainly not be held against him. "Everybody does the same thing" was the popular motto legitimizing the Serb crimes in Bosnia and elsewhere.

This ethnonational conception of modern Greece's identity also lies at the root of the difficulties religious and ethnic minorities have traditionally faced in Greece. As Mark Mazower puts it: "To the nationalist, minorities are always a potential fifth column: They are not a part of your national community, and the assumption is that they must be part of somebody else's."[13]

As far as the religious minorities are concerned, the identification of "Greekness" with Orthodoxy has had serious effects in the human rights domain: "The Greek worldview of society is an organic entity in which the ethnoreligious Greek ethnos, as embodied in the State, is the overriding integrative unit that dispenses with religious freedom for the non-Orthodox. Religious rights for minorities would threaten the integrity and purity of the Greek nation and state."[14]

The identification of Greekness with Orthodoxy, argues Dimitris Dimoulis, professor of political science at the University of Sao Paolo (Brazil), poses a very real threat to the members of other religious denominations. "A conflict of interests between the Orthodox Church and other Churches is viewed as a conflict between what is in the interest of the nation and what is against the nation."[15]

Whenever such a conflict of interests appears, the Greek Orthodox Church can always resort to a nationalist discourse and accuse the other religious minorities of failing to act in accordance with the national interests. That was the case during the winter of 1993, when a Catholic priest argued that the practice of including a person's religious denomination on Greek identity cards should be abolished, a move the Orthodox Church of Greece strongly opposes. In his reply to the priest, Archbishop Christodoulos— who at the time was the bishop of Dimitrias—accused the members of the small Catholic minority in the Cyclades Islands of siding with the enemy when Italy attacked Greece during World War II.[16]

Greece's religious minorities are viewed with suspicion not only by the Orthodox Church but also by the state. In the early 1990s it was revealed that the Greek Intelligence Service (EYP) had commissioned a study concerning the "dangers" posed by the activities of various religious groups in Greece. The study identified the Catholic Church and various Protestant and other churches (Pentecostals, Evangelists, Baptists, Unitarians, Mormons, and Jehovah's Witnesses) as dangerous groups. The EYP document divided Greeks into two categories: "authentic" Greeks, who follow the Orthodox creed, and "nonauthentic" ones who do not. "It would not be an overstatement to say that any Greek who is not Orthodox is not a real Greek. This criterion corresponds to the intuitions of our people who consider as 'traitors' the Greeks who have changed their faith."[17]

According to the study, "nonauthentic Greeks," constituted a threat to the well-being of Greek society: "The leaders and most of the followers of those organizations suffer from deficient national consciousness. This is due to the fact they obey foreign centers that control them." Catholics were deemed to be especially dangerous because of their proselytizing: "The Greek state and the Church must always be on the alert because the Vatican has not given up its efforts to latinize the Greeks."

The conceptions that underlie Greece's official policy toward ethnic minorities are also determined by the exclusivity of the Greek concept of the ethnos. Greece does not officially recognize the existence of ethnic minorities in its territories. The Turkish-speaking minority in Thrace is recognized only as a "religious" ("Muslim") minority, and the Greek state denies the existence of a Slav-Macedonian ethnic minority. Claims concerning the existence of minority languages face legal prosecution. On February 2, 2000, a criminal court in Athens awarded a fifteen-month jail sentence to a Greek citizen for promoting the Vlach language. The court convicted the man of "disseminating false information" that could "provoke public anxiety and give the impression that there are minority problems in Greece."[18] In general, any attempt by an ethnic group to claim recognition is generally perceived as being "foreign instigated" and against Greece's national interests.[19] This policy was succinctly summed up in July, 1999, by Parliamentary Speaker Apostolos Kaklamanis, who is also a leading member of the governing PASOK Party: "It is a well-known fact that in Greece there is no Turkish or Macedonian minority. There is a Muslim religious minority, which is respected. Any inventions that serve other purposes will be handled in the appropriate way."[20]

This official state policy can once again be traced to the logic of ethnic nationalism: "Since Greekness is an integral transcendent entity, non-Greeks are not—and cannot be—members of the ethnos. Hence they philosophically are not entitled to those rights that are available to members of the Greek ethnos."[21]

What is significant is that the perception that the existence of minorities constitutes a mortal danger to the nation has in some instances played a significant role in shaping Greek foreign policy. This was the case in Greece's conflict with Macedonia.[22] When former prime minister Constantine Mitsotakis stepped down, Greek policy toward the young republic had little to do with the issue of its name, as everybody had been led to assume. James Gow perceptively noted that the real bone of contention was Greece's "nonexistent" Slav-Macedonian minority. The main reason for Greece's obstinacy was the fact that the creation of a Macedonian state would have encouraged members of the minority in Greece to seek their collective rights.[23]

Mitsotakis himself confirmed this. Looking back, he claims that "from the first moment" he saw "the problem of Skopje in its true dimensions. What concerned me . . . was not the name of the State. The problem for me from the very beginning was that [we should not allow] the creation of a second minority problem in the area of Western Macedonia [in Greece]. My main aim was [to convince] the Republic [of Macedonia] to declare that there is no Slavomacedonian minority in Greece. This was the real key to our differences with Skopje."[24]

Greece's policy toward minorities, and particularly what is perceived as its negative attitude "toward the development of minority rights," obeys the logic of ethnonationalism.[25] According to Alexis Heraklides, who served from 1983 to 1997 as an expert on human rights issues in the Greek Foreign Ministry, Greece's policies were the result of the ideals of ethnic homogeneity that Greek ethnic nationalism espouses: "The domestic and international behavior of Greece in questions of minorities and human rights always creates the impression that she is afraid of those issues, that she has something to hide (her minorities or her behavior toward them) and that as a state and as a people Greece and the Greeks lack . . . the belief in the universality of values like human rights, which would also necessitate the respect of the 'Other'."[26]

Minorities, religious or ethnic, are perceived by the dominant ideology as being "alien" to the social body proper. This, as Mazower notes, is aptly symbolized by the fact that state documents on, for example, Greek Jews are not kept at the Ministry of the Interior, as is the case with the other citizens, but in the Ministry of Foreign Affairs.[27]

According to Ramet, a central feature of the most extreme form of ethnonationalism, namely chauvinism, consists in the predominance of the conspiratorial viewpoint in the public discourse. This ideological variant of nationalism focuses on the "promotion of a threat to the nation" and the "perpetuation of notions of hostile conspiracy."[28]

One of the distinctive features of Greece's overwhelming emotional support for Milošević's Serbia has been its intolerant and aggressive character. The same characteristics also marked the Greek people's reactions to any attempt by the world community to interfere in the mayhem in the former Yugoslavia. This aggression and intolerance could be seen in all public manifestations: in the media coverage and television talk shows, in the demonstrations against the embassies of NATO countries, in the protests that accompanied President Clinton's visit in October, 1999, and last, but by no means least, in the wave of terrorist attacks that took place in Greece against Western interests during the war in Kosovo.

According to Ramet, the psychological reactions that accompany various forms of nationalism are not accidental but derive from central structural features of the folk-worldview inherent in the nationalism in question.[29] Especially significant in this context is the dimension of the folk-worldview that relates to the perception of the world. When, for example, the international environment is perceived as indifferent or mixed, nationalism is toned down (Austrians, Slovenes, Canadians). When the international environment is perceived as beckoning, their nationalism takes an entrepreneurial form (Japanese, Italians). However, when the international environment is perceived as threatening, psychological reactions are characterized primarily by fear and aggression. The Greek worldview combines the idea that the country faces a constant threat and that it is at the same time the target of a huge conspiracy emanating predominantly from the West.

This can be seen in recent statements made by three of the most prominent members of Greek society: Pres. Kostis Stephanopoulos; composer Mikis Theodorakis, a Nobel Peace Prize candidate; and Archbishop Christodoulos.

The first was made in 1997, when President Stephanopoulos visited Mount Athos, one of the main centers of Orthodox monastic life. During his visit, the president, who is considered a political moderate, made a speech in which he denounced the "insidious threat" the West represented to Greece. This "threat," he said, was the result of the fact that the West was "inhabited by Protestants and Papists." Later in his speech he asked his audience to "forgive" the last Byzantine emperor for having asked for help from the Latins when the Ottomans seized Constantinople in 1453.[30]

Mikis Theodorakis made the second statement in an article he wrote for an Athens daily. In it, Theodorakis denounced NATO's intervention in Kosovo. However, in doing so he made no mention of the Serb repression of Kosovar Albanians or the ethnic cleansing taking place at the time. Theodorakis reaffirmed his belief that deep "historical and cultural differences" existed between Greece and the West, especially the "Five"—the French, British, Germans, Italians, and Americans—who he said despised and hated Greeks. He attributed all the national disasters that had befallen Greece during the past fifty years—from the Nazi occupation to the division of Cyprus—to the "Five."[31]

What did he perceive the insidious goals of the West to be? What did he think Westerners hoped to achieve by inflicting national disasters upon the

Greeks? The answer was obvious for all to see: "The West wants us to stop being Greeks, it wants to force us to change our faith."

Yet all was not lost. According to Theodorakis, the road to salvation passed through the cultural and national reawakening of the Greek nation. Greece should turn its back on the evil forces of Western materialism and seek spiritual succor from its Orthodox tradition. "The NATO airplanes," he wrote, "aim to extinguish the candles of the Good Friday's Lamentations and the light of the Resurrection." At the same time, he called upon Archbishop Christodoulos to lead Greece's "gigantic crusade" to its spiritual roots.

Greece's Nobel Peace Prize candidate pointed out that it would be hard for small countries like Greece or Serbia to stand up to the NATO war machine alone. He said they should therefore seek new international alliances. Humanity's hope, he wrote, lay in the creation of a military alliance with Russia, Belarus, and Ukraine—all Orthodox countries. Only their "nuclear deterrent" could put a stop to the evil machinations of NATO and the West against the Serbs and the Greeks. "If this [alliance] finally becomes real, the Russian army will automatically become the guardian of the borders of Yugoslavia."

Equally pronounced was the conspiratorial viewpoint that permeated Archbishop Christodoulos's speeches. Central in his discourse was the belief that his Greek Orthodox flock is always the target of conspiracies emanating from the West: "Our people feel that they are always being treated unjustly by the great and the powerful."[32] He said their feelings of enmity toward the West were justified by the fact that "the powerful of the Earth commit injustices against the Hellenes and ignore the rightful claims of Hellenism."[33] Moreover, the leader of the Greek Orthodox Church said the West is engaged in dark plots aimed at reducing the country's territorial size: "Our foreign friends are methodically trying to reduce the size of Greece."[34]

The common structure underlying all variants of such conspiracy theories posits the theme of the "victimization" of the Orthodox flock. Orthodox Greeks are constantly at the center of *"skotines sinomosies"* ("dark conspiracies") that emanate from *"xena kentra"* ("foreign centers"). All three of the prominent Greeks quoted above conceive of the West as an alien or enemy space. This "anti-Frankish" view constitutes an exact replica of the political geography that dominated the symbolic marking of space by the Orthodox populations of the Ottoman and Byzantine Empires.

Greek scholars who have studied the place and structure of conspiracy theories in contemporary Greek political discourse agree that they posit the division of the universe into two categories: the "friends of the Greeks" (philhellenes) and the "Greek haters" (mishellenes). According to this view, Greece is a nation "alone in the world." It is always surrounded by enemies. It always lives "on the edge of a crisis." Everywhere, conspiracies are being woven against it: They emanate from the "Ankara-Skopje-Tirana axis," from Washington, from Bonn, from London, from NATO, from the famous "Islamic arc," and, of course, from Turkey.[35]

Even more important than President Stephanopoulos's speech, Archbishop Christodoulos's sermons, or the Theodorakis article, were the reactions that followed—or rather that failed to follow. The worldview expressed in those statements was accepted by the overwhelming majority, as judged by the lack of reaction, as being self-evidently true, as reflecting the natural order of things. And perhaps it was—from the point of view of the local conceptual scheme, that is.

CHAPTER 9

The New Anti-Americanism

O ne of the events that marked popular discourse in Greece during the last decade was the rise of strong anti-American sentiments. In an opinion poll conducted among secondary school students at the end of the 1990s by the National Center of Social Research, respondents were asked to rank a number of nations from most to least popular. Americans joined Albanians and Turks at the bottom of the list—even lower than Gypsies, a people group that is not held in particularly high-esteem by Greeks. The Serbs were in first place.[1]

The first thing that must be noted is that this ideological configuration is a new phenomenon and as such should not be confused with earlier critiques of American policies. Conflating earlier and recent forms of anti-Americanism can lead to serious misinterpretation. This new ideological mutation developed to a large degree in response to events in neighboring Yugoslavia. However, it also exhibits structural features that will make it persist even after the Balkan crisis is over.

The ideology of anti-Americanism that marked the 1960s in Greece reflected the radical Left's state of mind. It based its critique of American policies on the inconsistency that purportedly existed between the ideals of liberty that Americans officially espoused and the policies they followed either at home—the so-called Jim Crow laws discriminating against blacks in the South—or abroad—supporting dictatorial regimes like the Greek military junta or the Pinochet regime in Chile. It also was an essentially benign philosophy. Despite its occasional violent rhetoric and acts, it did not challenge the essential principles upon which American society rested—

namely the principles of liberty, the rule of law and individual rights. What this ideology challenged was not the principles per se but their selective application. What it pointed out in its critique was that a country that was supposed to respect the rule of law and democratic procedures could not allow its secret services to cooperate in the overthrow of elected governments (as probably happened with the Allende government in Chile). Nor could its government acquiesce in the establishment of military dictatorships in NATO countries (as happened in Greece in 1967).[2]

The earlier form of ideological anti-Americanism differs in some very crucial respects from today's mutation. The first thing to be noted is that today's anti-Americanism is no longer the exclusive prerogative of the Left, as was the case in the 1960s. Today, both in Greece and elsewhere, its main advocates are to be found in equal proportions among the conservative Right, the communist Left, and the religious militants. These three streams are converging to form the great river of the "new anti-Americanism."

Greece's case is instructive. Conservative newspapers like *Vradini* or *Eleftheros Typos* denounce the United States with the same vehemence as the official Communist Party paper *Rizospastis*. A study conducted by the Department for the Study of Mass Media at Athens University revealed that anti-Americanism has become a common feature in conservative newspapers. At the same time, the study underlined that this fact is not restricted to the media but also characterizes the rhetoric of the political parties. The nationalistic anti-Americanism of Greek conservatives, the study claimed, converged with the traditional anti-Americanism of the Left. At the same time, "the anti-imperialist rhetoric of the PASOK government has been replaced by the nationalist rhetoric of the conservative forces."[3]

The underlying reasons for opposition to the United States often differ. The Greek Communist Party (one of the largest in the European Union), sees America as the "Great Satan" for the simple reason that U.S. policies precipitated the downfall of the Holy Soviet Empire. However, it is interesting to note that communist opposition to the United States today is no longer articulated only in the Marxist idiom but increasingly in the language of nationalism. Thus, the Communist Party strongly opposes any "U.S. dictated" rapprochement between Greece and Turkey.[4] At the same time, it is one of the staunchest defenders of the principle of "national sovereignty" and "territorial integrity." This new attitude has also affected the Communist Party's policy of relative tolerance toward the various ethnic minorities living in Greece. In July, 1999, when three Muslim parliamentary deputies from Thrace joined a number of NGOs in calling for Greek recognition of a "Macedonian" and a "Turkish" minority, General Secretary of the Communist Party Aleka Papariga rushed to denounce the initiative. She claimed the instigators sought to put pressure on Greece and "allow the U.S. to impose its own rules in the Greek-Turkish negotiations."[5]

The adoption of the nationalist viewpoint by the Greek Communist Party was cemented in the "National Front" strategy announced at the party's sixteenth congress in December, 2000. During her speech to party delegates, General Secretary Papariga said that the new strategy no longer included a precondition calling for other social agencies to accept socialism or worker power. The unity of the National Front would be grounded on the notions of the "defense of national sovereignty" and the rejection of "subservience to the demands of NATO and the U.S. and subjection to the New World Order and the Maastricht Treaty." She then reminded the delegates of the topicality and relevance of Stalin's dictum concerning the need "to raise the flag of national independence and national sovereignty."[6] The theoretical justification for this new strategy was provided in an article in the party's daily, *Rizospastis,* entitled: "Anti-Imperialist Struggles and Nationalism." The article made a distinction between "false nationalism" and "real patriotism." The latter, the author claimed, finds its true expression in the anti-imperialist internationalist struggle: "The masses have started making the transition from bourgeois nationalism to anti-imperialist patriotism."[7]

The Communist Party had already started putting in practice its anti-Western popular-front strategy during the period of the war in the former Yugoslavia. This took the form of participating in demonstrations against the U.S. embassy together with right-wing nationalists,[8] joining with "progressive forces" and organizing humanitarian convoys to Pale,[9] and organizing movements appealing to the Greek armed forces. The latter effort resulted in the creation of the Movement for National Defense under the auspices of the Communist Party in November, 2000. The speakers at the organization's first meeting included Adm. Christos Lymberis, former commander of the Greek armed forces; former admiral Gregory Demestichas; and former general George Alevromagiros. All three criticized NATO for supporting Turkey.[10]

From the very beginning, the Greek Communist Party was one of the most vocal opponents of NATO action during both the Bosnia and Kosovo wars because it "violated Serbian sovereignty" and aimed to "undermine Milošević."[11] One of the party's more noteworthy actions in this respect was the creation in November, 2000, of a Balkan Anti-NATO Center in Salonika whose aim was to coordinate anti-NATO activities in the region. Among those represented at the center were Milošević's Socialist Party, the Turkish Workers' Party, Bulgaria's Antifascist Union, the Marxist Platform of the Bulgarian Socialist Party, Georgi Dimitrof's Bulgarian Communist Party, and the Albanian Communist Party.[12]

The Greek Communist Party was also one of the Milošević regime's staunchest supporters, and in January, 2001, when Milošević's other political friends in Greece began to distance themselves from him, Aleka Papariga visited him in Belgrade to show her party's solidarity.

For some, the incorporation of nationalism into communist doctrine has a deeper ideological significance. "For the communist Left, the transition from communism to ethnic nationalism was not hard to make," argued Anna Damianidi in the left-leaning daily *Avghi*. "What is common in both systems is the total absence of a concept of freedom."[13] Nobel-laureate Friedrich Hayek made essentially the same point in *The Road to Serfdom* when he argued that nationalism can be seen as a form of socialism. In a similar vein, former U.S. ambassador to Yugoslavia Warren Zimmermann pointed out that the change that occurred in Yugoslavia in the late 1980s could be seen as a transition from one collectivist ideology, in this case communism, to another collectivist one, nationalism.[14] Both nationalism and communism can be seen as ideological mobilization machines for the fight against an ever-present enemy in whose name individual rights and freedoms are ruthlessly suppressed.

Some authors go so far as to argue that in specific historical cases the communist system was simply a more effective form of nationalism. Thus, John Lukacs has argued that Soviet communism was simply a veneer for Russian nationalism, and Stjepan Meštrović and his colleagues contend that Yugoslavian communism was a Trojan horse for the promotion of Serb national interests.[15]

The intellectual sources of the conservative Right's newly discovered anti-Americanism are rich and varied. In part they reflect the anti-Western and xenophobic attitude that characterizes the rhetoric and practices of the Greek Orthodox Church. However, it is important to understand the often-overlooked fact that it is not simply U.S. policy that offends the nationalist Right. It is the entire narrative of American society and history and the values that constitute it that contradict the basic premises of nationalist conservatism in Greece and perhaps elsewhere. Multicultural and multiethnic narratives challenge the very essence of linguistic, cultural, and ethnic homogeneity that have always constituted the pillars of Greek ethnonationalism.[16]

What must be noted here is that one of the main fears among conserva-

16. An effigy of President Clinton burns in Athens during the Kosovo crisis in the spring of 1999. Photo courtesy Eleftherotypia.

tive nationalists in Greece during the recent war in the Balkans was that the United States was trying to export its model of societal pluralism to the region. American support for Bosnia and Macedonia thus was interpreted by Greek conservatives as an attempt to export its multiethnic models to the Balkans.[17] If it is indeed the case, as Huntington argues, that the United States supported an independent Bosnia because of the multiethnic character of the latter, the exact opposite was the case with Greece, whose government maintained from the outset that Bosnia was doomed precisely because of its multiethnic character.[18]

Finally, as far as the Orthodox Church is concerned, its enmity toward the United States is part of the general militant anti-Western legacy of Eastern Orthodoxy.[19] The Greek Orthodox populations of the Ottoman Empire have always perceived the West as being inhabited by "barbarian Franks" or "Latins" or "schismatics" or "heretics." The religious bond that had cemented the Greek Orthodox population together for hundreds of years had always been strongly anti-Western. Nobody understood this better than Karl Marx, who in 1897 wrote: "There exists no polemical schism between the Musulmans and their Greek subjects; but the religious animosity against the Latins may be said to form the only common bond among the different races inhabiting Turkey and professing the Greek creed."[20]

*17. Thousands rally in Athens to protest President Clinton's visit to Greece in the fall of 1998.
Photo courtesy* Eleftherotypia.

The rhetoric employed by the Greek Orthodox Church when attacking the United States during the Kosovo war drew partly from the traditional conceptual framework of Eastern Orthodoxy: Thus America and its president were described as "Demon" or "Satan," and New York City was "the Whore of Babylon."[21] Archbishop Christodoulos, who also borrowed ideas from the discourse of the Left, made repeated references to U.S. "imperialism" while at the same time denouncing American ideas about a "New World Order" as being "similar to Nazi ones." Finally, he repeatedly attacked "globalization." "Resist, my dear Christians," he said. "The forces of globalization and religious marginalization are out to get us."[22]

It is also worth noting that the Greek archbishop recently said he finds the Communist Party of Greece's geopolitical views on issues like globalization, Kosovo, and U.S. foreign policy to be "much closer" to those of his church than those of many other political parties.[23] The convergence of the Greek Orthodox Church's positions with the communists' may not simply be an opportunistic alliance reflecting a specific political conjecture. Indeed, some very influential thinkers in the Greek Orthodox Church have recently argued that Orthodoxy represents the only true form of communism. Included in their ranks is Father George Metallinos, a theology professor at Athens University and an influential thinker and frequent guest on television talk shows. The persecution of the Orthodox Church in Russia by the Bolsheviks thus should not be seen as an attempt to impose by violent means a secular order of things, but rather as an attempt by "the German Kaiser's agent Lenin" to impose "false" communism in the country by destroying the "true" communism of the Orthodox Church.[24] The leader of the Communist Party of the Russian Federation, Gennadjii Zyuganov, has also stressed communism's need to be reinvigorated by returning to the protoreligious concept of *"obshchina"* (community).[25]

Finally, one of the most important elements fueling the Greek Church's strong anti-Western posture of the last several years has been the appearance of a group of influential "Neorthodox" thinkers who have revived and brought into focus the antagonism that existed between the Orthodox East and the Latin West during the Middle Ages. What these thinkers have done is recast traditional religious antagonisms in the contemporary idiom of world politics and use them as the basis for advocating foreign policy positions whose ultimate aim is the total separation of Greece from the West.

The most important among those thinkers is Christos Giannaras, a professor at Panteion University in Athens. His basic argument is that there is a fundamental conflict between the Orthodox tradition based on the communitarian ethos and Western Christianity, which stresses individualism, materialism, and conceptualism. However, what is more interesting for our purposes are his geopolitical views as expounded not only in his books but also in many newspaper articles and columns.[26]

According to Giannaras, Greece has nothing to gain from its contacts with the West. For him, the West is inferior, corrupt, and dominated by extreme political amoralism. The crimes the West has committed—the "slaughtering of the Serbs" or its support for the suppression of the rights of Turkish Kurds, for example—are due to its instrumental rationalism, which leads to a dehumanization of its foreign policy. Moreover, he says, the West continues to perpetuate the legacy of hatred for the Orthodox Church that started with the schism and the Filioque dispute and culminated with the sacking of Constantinople by the Crusaders. Western hatred is primarily directed toward the Greeks not only because of their religious beliefs but also because they are the inheritors of the Byzantine Empire. The West, particularly the United States, has been trying continuously to undermine Greek interests by helping Greece's enemies—including Turkey, "Skopje," the Bosnian Muslims, and the Albanians. Greece has been subjected to the "ultimate degradation" of having to rely on the West for its continued existence by pleading for Western protection against the Turks.

According to Giannaras, all the misfortunes that have befallen Greeks during their recent history—from the Asia Minor catastrophe in 1922 to the Turkish invasion of Cyprus in 1974 and the resulting division of the island—were due to Greece's failed attempt to imitate the West. The Greeks' "fall" will not end until they realize their superiority as members of the Orthodox Church. The rot will stop only when Greeks substitute the "servility" that characterizes their relationship with the West with the spirit of resistance against the latter's "immoral barbarism." Herein lies Greece's path to salvation and moral rejuvenation.

Let us note briefly at this point certain similarities that characterize the developments of the Orthodox ideology in Greece with, on one hand, Muslim fundamentalism as expressed by Sayyid Qutb, and Jewish-Zionist fundamentalism as expressed by Zeev Jabotinsky and Chief Rabbi Avraam Yitzak Kook on the other.

The Greek Orthodox fundamentalism shares a similar conception of the West with Muslim fundamentalism, which also sees the West as an immoral, unjust, and unfair society. The Western world has, according to this view, lost its moral compass. It promotes only blind egoism and violence in interpersonal relations. A society based on solidarity, community, love, social justice, and morality presupposes a total rejection of the Western model.[27]

Greek Orthodox ideology shares similar conceptions concerning the uniqueness of its flock with Jewish-Zionist fundamentalism. The Jews are not simply a nation like all other nations (as argued by traditional Zionism) but the "Chosen People" who, through suffering and pain, will relive their glorious past and recreate "Greater Israel." Through this process the "Chosen People" will save humanity from moral decay.[28]

Seen as a system of ideas, the new anti-Americanism constitutes one more variant of the dominant ideology of ethnonationalism in Greece. As such, it has very little in common with the critiques of American policies and social structures that were prevalent in the 1960s and early 1970s. The latter were rights-based discourses and had emancipation as their goal. The new-anti-Americanism, on the other hand, stresses closure, irrationality, and occasionally blind hate. Popular Greek composer Mikis Theodorakis made one of the most extreme statements articulating this new position in the summer of 1999. During the course of an interview he said: "I hate Americans and everything American. I hope that the youth will begin to hate everything American."[29]

Theodorakis, who also happened to be a close friend of Slobodan Milošević and was occasionally ferried around in the latter's private plane, had by that time already become immensely popular by stating during a press conference that "there is no difference between Hitler, Clinton, and Blair."[30]

Confusing the two forms of anti-Americanism means committing what philosophers call "a category mistake," which in some cases may have serious policy implications. That was the case with President Clinton's visit to Greece in October, 1999. His trip planners thought that if he made a speech in Athens condemning American support to the military junta that ruled Greece from 1967–74, he would placate the Greeks protesting his visit. It did not work. The massive and violent demonstrations against his visit went ahead as planned. What President Clinton's advisers failed to understand was that the reactions to his visit were motivated at a deeper level by the new form of anti-Americanism, which had little if anything in common with older forms. The people protesting Clinton's visit were not the same individuals that had carried the banner of resistance to the usurpation of political freedoms by the military junta in the late 1960s. These masses instead were affirming the return to the homeostasis of a Balkan society marked by communal bonding, religious solidarity, and the pervasiveness of tribal worldview.

Conclusion

G reece's identification with the policies of Milošević, Karadžić, Mladić, Arkan, and the rest; the indifference with which local public opinion greeted every new horror committed in Bosnia or Kosovo; the rise of an Orthodox militant nationalism; the intense feelings of hate projected against the West and especially the United States—all those reactions took many in the West by surprise. They were certainly not expected from a country most observers believed had been fully integrated into two of the most central Western institutions, namely the EU and NATO.

What the pundits predicted at the close of the 1980s was the exact opposite of what actually happened. "The prospects of Greece," wrote a leading Greek foreign-policy analyst, "appeared bright at the end of 1990. The most stable, affluent, democratic, and well-connected with the West state in the region, it was ideally suited to play the role of the honest broker in the Balkans."[1] They were convinced that Greece, having the advantages of being economically more developed than its Balkan neighbors and a member of the EU, would surely play a leading role in helping the other Balkan countries that had recently emerged from the traumatic experience of communism drag themselves out of the proverbial "Balkan darkness."

What happened instead, contrary to all predictions, was that Greece gleefully jumped into that darkness with both feet. As Adam Nicolson wrote in the *Spectator:* "Greece, from being one of us since the war, has become one of them (Balkans)."[2] Instead of trying to promote the Western gospel of human rights, free markets, and political democracy, Greece opted for the discourse of ethnic nationalism and religious militancy. Instead of opposing

Milošević's bullying of the Serb democratic opposition at home and Slovenia, Croatia, Bosnia, and Kosovo abroad, Greece chose to side with the Belgrade regime, thereby rendering itself vulnerable to international criticism as being, in Noel Malcolm's words, another "Bully of the Balkans."³ Judging from the reports that were appearing in the international media during the early and middle 1990s, Greece's positive image, so carefully nourished by its modernizing political and economic elites, was beginning to collapse like a house of cards.

Among the most negative articles published in the Western press at the time were two London *Times* editorials. The first claimed that Greece was "the least free society," whereas the other called Greece "the least pleasant European country [in which] to live."⁴ An editorial in London's *Sunday Telegraph* advocated Greece's expulsion from the EU.⁵

In an interview aired July 15, 2001, on the Greek radio station *Flash,* Petar Luković, one of the leading Serb opposition journalists, summed up Greece's policies toward Serbia during the nineties as follows:

I think that during the last ten years, the role of Greece was very important. Its policy did not benefit the Serbian people, but exclusively the Milošević regime, helping the Milošević family and its associates retain power in Belgrade. I will be very blunt and very brutal. I think Greece played a shameful role. It was used throughout this period by the [Milošević] regime as a fine example of a country that supported democratic and patriotic Serbia. The famous 'Greek-Serbian friendship' was simply a mask or the framework which allowed the Milošević family to obtain support from the Greek government. Throughout those years, Milošević was criticized by the Greek government only once or twice. Both Greek and Serbian politicians agreed on the use of nationalism as a means for staying in power. I still remember all those rallies in Greece in support of Milošević . . . . It is very hard for someone who had been in the Serbian democratic opposition to understand why Greece—not just its government officials but all the political parties—supported a person whom we knew already at the time to be a war criminal, a person who started the war in Bosnia and Croatia. Greeks should ask themselves why they wasted ten years in supporting something that was paranoid, primitive, and criminal from the very beginning.

Greece's response to the new Balkan wars showed once again that the Westernizing experiment that had started in the nineteenth century was over and what Paschalis Kitromilides called the "old problem" of the incomplete liberal transformation of the country's ideology continued to persist. What was even more curious was the fact that Greece's process of gradual disengagement (mental not institutional) from the West was taking place at a time of economic growth and technological modernization in the country. Yet as Huntington has argued, and as the case of Greece seemed to prove, economic growth and modernization do not necessarily lead to Westernization. On the contrary, modernization seemed to reduce the West's power.[6] The average Greek citizen was not becoming more susceptible to the teachings of Immanuel Kant or John Locke simply because he happened to hold a mobile phone in his hand or because he was sporting Gucci loafers.

Strangely, the exact opposite seemed to be happening. Economic growth and modernization seemed to be leading Greece farther away from the West. Behind the facade of work lunches and power breakfasts that Greek ministers and businessman held with their European counterparts in Brussels, lay a deep conceptual divide that separated Greece from the West. This gap pertained especially to the domain of human rights. In Greece, names like Srbrenica, Goražde, Foća, and Omarska, meant (and mean) practically nothing. They never entered the chain of signifiers that characterize the discourse of the trend-setting intellectuals in the West.

This was not a new phenomenon. In Greece, rights-based discourses had always been conspicuously absent. Events like the Soviet Gulag, the "killing fields" of Kampuchea, or the Eastern European dissident movement—which marked the discourse of the chattering classes in the West during the 1970s and 1980s—never really entered the discourse of political critique in Greece.[7]

What was interesting about the protests against the U.S. president during his visit to Athens in the fall of 1999 was not the protests per se, but the fact that no such protests occurred when Greece was hosting leaders whose human rights records were extremely problematic. During the past twenty years visitors to Greece have included—apart from indicted war criminals Radovan Karadzić and Slobodan Milošević—dictators like Romania's Nikolai Ceausescu, East Germany's Erich Honnecker, Libya's Muammar Qadhafi, Bulgaria's Todor Zhivkov, and other unseemly characters.[8] Not only had all these celebrities been given the red carpet treatment by the Greek political class, not a single demonstration ever took place protesting their presence.

Culture and nationalist ideology had been much more potent in forming the "habits of the heart" of Greek society than economy or technological modernization. If one scratched the surface of social life, one would find behind the facade of cosmopolitan chatter that echoed in the chic cafes of Kolonaki a country that for many years had been in the grip of a virulent ethnic nationalism promoted predominantly by an alliance of the communist Left, the nationalist Right, and the Orthodox Church of Greece. Furthermore, it was an ethnic nationalism whose content was intensely anti-Western.

Cornelius Castoriadis, the country's most prominent postwar social thinker, delivered the harshest assessment of Greece's behavior during the Bosnia war. A few years before his death in 1997, Castoriadis asserted that the Serbs crimes were being covered up in Greece by a campaign of lies and propaganda which presented the Serb "brethren" as victims of plots engineered in the Vatican, by the Germans, and so forth. "In my eyes," he said, "the Greek politicians, the journalists, the people who work at the media, and the others who are responsible for this campaign of disinformation are moral accomplices in the cover-up of the Serb crimes in Croatia and Bosnia."[9]

However, the state of affairs Castoriadis described should not be interpreted as resulting from the fact that Greece and Serbia share the same religion. Nor should Greece's dissenting vis-à-vis its Western partners' policies be seen as evidence of a division between Eastern and Western Christendom.

The Greek-Serb alliance was not "holy." It was an "unholy alliance" emanating from the secular ideology of nationalism. The reasons for the Greek "abnormality" within the West should not be sought in the realms of church and religion but rather in the realms of state and nation building. The Orthodox Church in Greece is not a "religious" but a political institution, having been totally "nationalized" during the last century. Its role has consisted less in the salvation of souls than in the creation of the ideological preconditions that would ensure the cultural homogeneity of the Greek nation.

"The Orthodox Church of Greece," writes Dimitris Dimoulis, "constructs its identity as Orthodox and Christian, i.e., as anti-Western and anti-Turkish. It thus assumes from the very start an ethnoconstructive function." To carry out this function, the Orthodox Church of Greece is protected and financed by the state. At the same time, "those that are not members of the Greek Orthodox Church are not simply viewed as belonging to a different faith, but are immediately stigmatized as being 'anti-Greek' and therefore suspect."[10]

The relevant division thus is not between Eastern Orthodoxy and Western Christendom. It is between Greek ethnic nationalism versus the civic nationalisms one finds to a greater or lesser degree in the West. The discourse of ethnic nationalism that dominates Greek society played a crucial role in the popular responses to the mayhem in the former Yugoslavia. By turning the Bosnian Muslims and Kosovo Albanians into "others," it facilitated the process of blocking them out of the space of the moral representations through which Greek society viewed and evaluated what was happening in there.

When Greek society was confronted with the tragic events in the former Yugoslavia, the absence from the political culture of the country of concepts related to the moral autonomy of the individual (individual rights, the rule of law, and so forth) played a determining role in the way its citizens responded. There was no human rights capital to be tapped by the Greek society, either by its population or by its elites. This accounts for the fact that Greece remains entrapped within a classical Balkan problematic, even though it appears to be totally oriented toward the West because of its economic ties with the European Union.[11]

Will Greece stay trapped in this problematic? Will she continue adhering to the logic of ethnic nationalism? The answer to that question depends on the answer to the more general theoretical question: Can ethnic nationalism transform itself into a civic variant?

Notes

Introduction: The Setting

1. *Eleftherotypia,* Oct. 2, 1995.
2. Victoria Clark, *Why Angels Fall,* 123.
3. *Eleftherotypia,* (left of center), *Kathimerini* (conservative), and *To Vima* (center).
4. Former prime minister Constantine Mitsotakis; Foreign Ministers Antonis Samaras, Karolos Papoulias, and Michalis Papakonstantinou; the present foreign minister, George Papandreou; and the former deputy foreign minister, Virginia Tsouderou.
5. To mention those that come immediately to mind: I. Kanellis, G. Pretenteris, R. Someritis, D. Psichogios, S. Kouloglou, M. Moronis, K. Tsapogas, L. Chatziprodromidis, V. Georgakopoulou, T. Papadopoulou, S. Polimilis, N. Voulelis, Ios, A. Papandropoulos, A. Papagianidis, G. Mitralias, G. Kapopoulos, G. Loverdos, C. Poulidou, K. Karis, G. Pantazopoulos, T. Georgakopoulos, G. Aggelopoulos, K. Mitsios, S. Telloglou, G. Tzanetakos, A. Papachilas, F. Gergeles, and S. Theodorakis.
6. Alexis de Tocqueville, *Democracy in America,* 1:299. For bringing this term into the focus of contemporary sociological analysis, see Stjepan G. Meštrović, *The Balkanization of the West,* 1:139–41.
7. For this distinction, see Uffe Ostergaard, *Tocqueville og de moderne analyser af den amerikanske nationalkarakter og politiske kultur.*
8. Jacques Derrida, *Of Grammatology.*
9. Tom Nairn, *Faces of Nationalism,* 105.
10. Sabrina P. Ramet, *Social Currents in Eastern Europe,* 454.
11. Samuel Huntington, *The Clash of Civilizations and the Remaking of World Order.*
12. Ibid., 125.
13. Ibid., 26.
14. Ibid., 162.
15. Ibid., 163.
16. Glenny, *Fall of Yugoslavia,* 182.
17. Quoted in *Eleftherotypia,* Oct. 2, 1995.
18. Quoted in ibid, May 10, 1994.
19. Sabrina P. Ramet, *Nihil Obstat,* 48.
20. Louis Althusser, *Politics and History.*

21. "Greece's veneration of the Serbs," noted Professor Heraklides of Panteion University of Athens, "was unique during the 1990s. Neither Russia nor any other Balkan Orthodox country exhibited such an attitude" (Alexis Heraklides, *I Ellada kai o "Ex anatolon Kindinos,"* 4).

22. Ramet, *Nihil Obstat*, 48.

23. Nikiforos P. Diamantouros, "Ellinismos kai Ellinikotita," in *Ellinismos kai Ellinikotita*, ed. D. Tsaousis; Thanos Lipowatz, "Orthodoxos Christianismos kai Ethnikismos," *Hellenic Review of Political Science* 2 (1993): 31–48; Heraklides, *I Ellada kai o "Ex anatolon Kindinos"*; Peter F. Sugar, "External and Domestic Roots of Eastern European Nationalism," in *Nationalism in Eastern Europe*, ed. Peter F. Sugar and Ivo John Lederer; William W. Hagen, "The Balkan's Lethal Nationalism," *Foreign Affairs* 78, no. 4 (1999): 52–65; Roger Brubaker, *Nationalism Reframed*.

24. For a discussion of these distinctions, see Ernest Gellner, *Nationalism;* John Hutchinson, *Modern Nationalism;* Anthony D. Smith, *The Ethnic Origins of Nations;* and John Breuilly, "Approaches to Nationalism," in *Mapping the Nation*, ed. Gopal Balakrisnam, 146–74.

25. Smith, *Ethnic Origins of Nations*, 136.

26. Glenda Sluga, "Identity Gender and the History of European Nations and Nationalism," *Nations and Nationalism* 4, no. 1 (1998): 88.

27. Lipowatz, "Orthodoxos Christianismos," 54–58; Elli Skopotea, *To "Protypo Vasilio" kai I Megali Idea;* Roderick Beaton, "Romanticism in Greece" in *Romanticism in National Context*, ed. Roy Porter and Mikulas Teich, 92–108.

28. Adamantia Pollis, "Ellada: Ena Provlimatiko Kosmiko Kratos," in *Nomika Zitimata Thriskeftikis Eterotitas stin Ellada*, ed. Dimitris Christopoulos, 168–69.

29. Ramet, *Nihil Obstat*, 162.

30. Tom Nairn, "Cyprus and the Theory of Nationalism," in *Small States in the Modern World*, ed. Peter Worsley and Paschalis Kitromilides.

31. Adamantia Pollis, *Kratos, Dikaio kai, Antrhropina Dikaiomata stin Ellada*, 151

32. Mark Mazower, *The Balkans*, 105.

33. Paschalis Kitromilides, *Enlightenment, Nationalism, and Orthodoxy*, 77.

34. Ibid., 78.

35. Ibid., 65.

36. Nikiforos P. Diamantouros and Stephen E. Larrabee, "Democratization in South-Eastern Europe," in *Experimenting with Democracy*, ed. Geoffrey Pridham and Tom Gallagher, 28–36.

37. Sabrina P. Ramet "The Serbian Church and the Serbian Nation," in *Beyond Yugoslavia*, ed. Sabrina P. Ramet and Ljubiša S. Admamović, 101–23.

38. Stepjan G. Meštrović, ed., *Genocide After Emotion*, 11.

Chapter 1. "United Like a Fist!"

1. The quote used as the chapter title comes from a statement by Vladislav Jovanović, foreign minister of the Former Republic of Yugoslavia, in Athens in April, 1994.

2. *Ethnos*, July 13, 1995.

3. Ibid., Aug. 8, 1995.

4. Ibid., July 13, 1995.

5. Ibid., Aug. 20, 1995.

6. *Eleftherotypia,* July 23, 1995.

7. *Ethnos,* Aug. 2, 1995.

8. Quoted in *Eleftherotypia,* July 8, 1993.

9. Quoted in *Ethnos,* Aug. 20, 1995.

10. Quoted on a talk show aired by popular television station SKY in August, 1995. A full transcript was published in the weekly *Chrisi Avgi,* Sept. 8, 1995.

11. Quoted in *Eleftheri Ora,* Sept. 25, 1995.

12. Antischolio, *Srebrenica,* 199.

13. Ibid., 220.

14. Quoted in *Eleftherotypia,* April 17, 1994. Papandreou, leader of the socialist PASOK Party, served as Greece's prime minister from 1981–89 and from 1993–96. He died in Athens in 1996 at the age of seventy-seven.

15. Quoted in *Eleftherotypia,* Dec. 21, 1994.

16. Quoted in *Eleftherotypia,* Dec. 20, 1994. Mitsotakis was leader of the conservative New Democracy (ND) Party. He served as prime minister of Greece from 1990–1993, when his party lost the elections to PASOK. He considers himself to be one of Milošević's close friends.

17. Ibid., Dec. 27, 1994.

18. Ibid., Dec. 21, 1994.

19. Ibid., May 15, 1993. Archbishop Serapheim was the leader of the Greek Orthodox Church from 1974–1988. He died in April, 1988, while still in office.

20. *Ethnos,* May 9, 1994.

21. For relations between the Church and the military junta, see Giorgos Karagiannis, *Eklissia kai Kratos,* and Giorgos Moustakis, *I Genesi toy Christianofasismoy stin Ellada.*

22. Antischolio, *Srebrenica,* 220.

23. *Piraiki Eklisia,* Apr., 1995, 42–43.

24. Antischolio, *Srebrenica,* 208.

25. Quoted in Laura Silber and Allan Little, *Yugoslavia,* 246.

26. *Eleftherotypia,* Jan. 18, 1995.

27. *Apogevmatini,* June 15, 1993; *Ta Nea,* June 15, 1993.

28. Quoted in *Eleftherotypia,* June 15, 1993.

29. Aris Mousionis, taped interview with author, Salonika, Apr. 9, 2001.

30. Quoted in *Eleftherotypia,* June 15, 1993.

31. Quoted in *Apogevmatini,* June 15, 1993.

32. *Ethnos,* May 15, 1993.

33. *Eleftherotypia,* Aug. 10, 1993.

34. Ibid., Mar. 9, 1994.

35. Ibid., Jan. 21, 1994.

36. *Eleftherotypia,* June 16, 1993.

37. For Milošević's comings and goings to Athens, see Sabrina P. Ramet "The Macedonian Enigma," in *Beyond Yugoslavia,* ed. Ramet and Adamović.

38. *Eleftherotypia,* Dec. 18, 2000.

39. Quoted in the *Wall Street Journal* (European ed.), Aug. 9, 1996 (hereafter *WSJE*).

40. Antischolio, *Srebrenica,* 191–203.

41. *Eleftherotypia,* May 23, 1995.

42. Ibid., Dec. 8, 1993.

43. Antischolio, *Srebrenica,* 209.

44. Leonidas Chatziprodromidis, *I Dolofonia tis Yougoslavias,* 23.

45. Ibid.

46. Saša Mirković, taped interview with author, Nov., 2000.

47. Quoted in *Eleftherotypia,* Sept. 21, 1995.

48. Quoted in Chatziprodromidis, *I Dolofonia tis Yougoslavias,* 281.

49. Mirković interview.

50. Quoted in Antischolio, *Srebrenica,* 203.

51. Ibid.

52. Quoted in Takis Michas, "Greece Keeps Dismissing Serb Atrocities," *WSJE,* Aug. 22, 1995.

53. For anti-Turkish views in the Greek educational system, see Anna Fragoudaki et al., *Ti ine I Patrida Mas? Ethnokentrismos stin Ekpaidevsi;* in Greek political culture, see Heraklides, *I Ellada kai o "Ex anatolon Kindinos";* in the Greek media, see John Carr, "Manufacturing the Enemy: Nationalism and Turkophobia in the Greek Media as a Cultural and Economic Phenomenon" (master's thesis, Leicester University, n.d.).

54. See also Mark Almond, *Europe's Backyard War.*

55. *Eleftherotypia,* Mar. 17, 1991.

56. Quoted in ibid., Mar. 8, 1996.

57. Quoted in ibid., Dec. 16, 1994.

58. Quoted in ibid., Dec. 4, 1994.

59. Quoted in Antischolio, *Srebrenica,* 198.

60. Ibid.

61. *Eleftherotypia,* May 23, 1995.

62. Ibid., Mar. 3, 1995.

63. Ibid.

64. Takis Michas, "Greece Questions the War Crimes Tribunal," *WSJE,* Aug. 9, 1996.

65. *Adesmeftos Tipos,* May 6, 1995.

66. *Eleftherotypia,* May 27, 1995.

67. Michas, "Greece Keeps Dismissing Serb Atrocities."

68. *Eleftherotypia,* Feb. 29, 1996.

69. *I Thessalia,* Feb. 21, 1993.

70. *Ependitis,* May 30, 1993.

71. *Kathimerini,* June 26, 1993.

72. *To Vima,* Mar. 31, 1993.

73. *Ta Nea,* June 17, 1993.

74. *Eleftherotypia,* Dec. 21, 1995.

75. *WSJE,* May 9, 1996.

76. *Eleftherotypia,* Jan. 20, 2001.

77. Alexis Heraklides, *I Ellada kai o "Ex anatolon Kindinos,"* 78–79. See also Misha Glenny, *The Fall of Yugoslavia,* 165.

78. *Eleftherotypia,* July 14, 1995. Papoulias, a close collaborator of Andreas Papandreou, served as foreign minister in the PASOK governments in 1985–89 and again in 1993–96.

79. Quoted in ibid., Dec. 2, 1994.

80. Quoted in ibid., June 14, 1993.

81. Aris Mousionis, taped interview with author, Thessaloniki, May, 2001. Mousionis says that his change of heart took place during the summer of 1995 while he was in Bosnia: "I had firsthand reports about what happened in Goražde, Tuzla, and above all Srbrenica. I felt that after that there was no longer any higher anti-imperialist ideal that could justify those horrors."

82. Quoted in *Eleftherotypia,* Dec. 9, 1996.

83. *Liberation,* Nov. 30, 1993.

84. See, for example, *Eleftherotypia,* May 8, 1998.

85. Mousionis interview.

86. Quoted in Michas, "Greece Keeps Dismissing Serb Atrocities."

87. Quoted in Michas, "Greece Questions the War Crimes Tribunal."

88. Ibid.

89. See, for example, Christos Rozakis's "Ta Adiexoda Stereotipa tis Ellinikis Exoterikis Politikis" in *Se Anazitizi Exoterikis Politikis.*

90. Takis Michas, "Another Blow to Peace Prospects in Cyprus," *WSJE,* Jan. 8, 1997.

Chapter 2. Plans for Macedonia

1. The term *Macedonia* is adopted for reasons of brevity for the state whose official name is the Former Yugoslav Republic of Macedonia.

2. Quoted in *Eleftherotypia,* Sept. 19, 1993.

3. For the Greek view on Macedonia, see Theodoros Couloumbis and Sotiris Dalis, *I Elliniki Exoteriki Politi sto Katofli toy 21ou Aiona;* Evangelos Kofos, "The Macedonian Question: The Politics of Mutation," *Balkan Studies* (1986); *The Macedonian Affair: A Historical Review of Attempts to Create a Counterfeit Nation;* and Michalis Papakonstantinou, *To Imerologio enos Poltikou.*

4. *Guardian* (UK), Jan. 31, 1992.

5. Nicos P. Mouzelis, *O Ethnikismos stin Isteri Anaptiksi,* 55.

6. Pavlos Sarlis, *The Break-Up of Yugoslavia,* 224.

7. Kofos, "Macedonian Question," 159.

8. Loring Danforth, *The Macedonian Conflict,* 12. See also Christopher Bennett, *Yugoslavia's Bloody Collapse,* 218–21.

9. Neophytos Loizidis, "Greece and the Macedonian Problem after the Interim Accord of September 1995" (Ph.D. diss, Central European University, Budapest and Warsaw, 1998), 11.

10. Danforth, *Macedonian Conflict,* 34.

11. Giorgos Babiniotis, ed., *I Glossa tis Makedonias.* "Skopje" is used frequently in Greece to refer to Macedonia. Similarly, the Macedonian language is called "Skopjana," and the nation's inhabitants are called "Skopjani."

12. Quoted in Alexandros Tarkas, *Athina-Skopje: Piso apo tis Klistes Portes,* 31. Samaras served as foreign minister from 1989 to 1992, when he resigned because he disagreed with Prime Minister Mitsotakis over the Macedonia issue.

13. *Greece: Free Speech on Trial. Government Stifles Dissent on Macedonia.*

14. Quoted in Tarkas, *Athina-Skopje,* 120–21.

15. It is perhaps worth noting that this document was designated for internal use and was not to be leaked to the media.

16. Quoted in Theodore Skilakakis, *Sto Onoma tis Makedonias,* 259.

17. See, for example, D. Andersen's article in the *WSJE,* Feb. 21, 1992; Eric Hobsbawm's articles in *The Nation,* Aug. 31 and Sept. 7, 1992; and William Pfaff, "Reflections," *New Yorker,* Aug. 10, 1992, 69.

18. See chapter 9.

19. Center for Preventive Action, *Toward Comprehensive Peace in Southeast Europe,* 37.

20. Ibid., 38.

21. See Fred A. Reed, *Salonica Terminus;* and Danforth, *Macedonian Conflict.*

22. This was revealed in the briefings given journalists by Western diplomats, as well as in the alarmist tone of most news items appearing in the Western media during that period. See Victoria Clark, *Why Angels Fall,* 146; Manos M. Iliadakis, *Apo to Makedoniko sti Nea Taxi kai sto Skopiano,* 325–73; and the conclusion of this book.

23. Antischolio, *Srebrenica,* 160.

24. Quoted in Tarkas, *Athina-Skopje,* 34.

25. Quoted in ibid., 35.

26. For a comparison of the use of minorities for destabilization purposes by Nazi Germany and Milošević's Serbia, see Bennett, *Yugoslavia's Bloody Collapse,* 243.

27. Ibid., 219.

28. Quoted in Skilakakis, *Sto Onoma tis Makedonias,* 259.

29. *The Macedonian Affair,* 6.

30. See Alex Dragnitch, *Serbs and Croats.*

31. Tarkas, *Athina-Skopje,* 37.

32. Ibid., 135–36.

33. Ibid., 136–37.

34. Quoted in ibid., 143.

35. Quoted in Skilakakis, *Sto Onoma tis Makedonias,* 116.

36. Tarkas, *Athina-Skopje,* 146.

37. *Eleftherotypia,* Jan. 11, 1992.

38. Quoted in Antischolio, *Srebrenica,* 152. Virginia Tsouderou served as deputy foreign minister under the ND government from 1991–93.

39. Quoted in Someritis, 1992.

40. Quoted in Antischolio, *Srebrenica,* 147. Raznatović was murdered in January, 2000, in Belgrade.

41. Aggelos Elefantis, "Apo tin Ethnikistiki Exarsi sto Perithorio," in *O Ianos tou Ethnikismou ke i Elliniki Valkaniki Politiki,* ed. Aggelos Elefantis et al., 58.

42. Quoted in *Eleftherotypia,* July 22, 1993.

43. Thomas Halverson, "The U.S. Perspective," in *International Perspectives on the Yugoslav Conflict,* ed. Alax Danchev and Thomas Halverson, 19.

44. *Eleftherotypia,* Feb. 20, 1994. For a different and intriguing interpretation of Papandreou's reasons for imposing the embargo, see chapter 3.

45. Kiro Gligorov, interview with author, June 12, 2001.

Chapter 3. The Blame Game

1. For more on this "disinformation machine," see Almond, *Europe's Backyard War*, 355.

2. Quoted in *Eleftherotypia*, Mar. 21, 1994.

3. David Owen, *Balkan Odyssey*, 261. The abbreviation COREU refers to the *Correspondence européene* telex network, which allows member nations to transmit encrypted messages containing confidential information.

4. Quoted in an interview on the Greek radio station Flash, Mar. 3, 2001.

5. Quoted in *Eleftherotypia*, Feb. 15, 1994 .

6. Quoted in ibid., Feb. 19, 1994.

7. Ibid., Feb. 20, 1994.

8. *Sunday Telegraph* (London), Dec. 11, 1995.

9. Papakonstantinou, *To Imerologio enos Politkou*, 117. Papakonstantinou served as foreign minister in Constantine Mitsotakis's ND government from August, 1992, to October, 1993.

10. Owen, *Balkan Odyssey*, 75.

11. James Gow, "British Perspectives," in *International Perspectives*, ed. Danchev and Halverson, 87–89.

12. Owen, *Balkan Odyssey*, 5.

13. *Eleftherotypia*, Feb. 3, 1994.

14. "How Can They Sleep at Night?" Amnesty International Report October EUR 63/22/97, Oct., 1997, Amnesty International, London.

15. Maria N. Todorova, *Imagining the Balkans*, 138–39.

16. "How Can They Sleep at Night?" Janko Janjić was killed on Oct. 13, 2000, when a hand grenade he was carrying detonated as UN peacekeepers tried to arrest him.

17. *WSJE*, Sept. 24, 1997.

18. Meštrović, *Balkanization of the West*, 97.

19. Suzan L. Woodward, *Balkan Tragedy*, 223.

20. Quoted in *Eleftherotypia*, Jan. 13, 2001.

Chapter 4. The Spirit of Enterprise

1. *Eleftherotypia*, Oct. 24, 1995.

2. Quoted in ibid., July 6, 1999.

3. Ibid., Oct. 6, 2000.

4. Quoted in Parliamentary Gazette, Feb. 6, 1997. When I visited Tzoumakas in the ministry a few days later and asked him why no one in the cabinet had objected to Papandreou's plan, he looked at me as if I was coming from another planet: "Nobody ever said no to Papandreou!" he replied.

5. Quoted in *WSJE*, June 15, 1996.

Chapter 5. Hating the "Franks"

1. "Franks" was the collective name the Orthodox populations of the Ottoman and Byzantine Empires used for inhabitants of the Latin West.

2. United Press International, "Violence Marks Clinton's Greece Visit," Nov. 19, 1999.

3. See chapter 9.

4. Nikos Dimou in *Ethnos,* Nov. 14, 1999.

5. *Ta Nea,* Nov. 20, 1999.

6. *Eleftherotypia,* Nov. 25, 1999.

7. Quoted in ibid., Mar. 26, 1999.

8. Quoted in ibid., May 19, 1999.

9. Quoted in ibid., Apr. 24, 2000.

10. Quoted in ibid., Mar. 29, 1999.

11. *WSJE,* Apr. 14, 1999.

12. Quoted in *Eleftherotypia,* Apr. 6, 1999.

13. See Christoforos Vernardakis, ed., *I Koini Gnomi stin Ellada,* 81–113.

14. Gustav Auernheimer, "Der Kosovokonflict und die Griechishe Offentlichkeit," *In Südosteuropa* 48 (July–Aug., 1999): 391.

15. *To Vima,* Apr. 29, 1999.

16. Quoted in *Athens News,* Apr. 6, 1999.

17. Karin Hope, private communication with author, May 10, 1999.

18. *Eleftherotypia,* Mar. 20, 1999.

19. See "Greek soldiers accuse Govt of preparing to send 800-strong army to Kosovo," http://balkanunity.demon.co.uk/serbia/soldiers.html.

20. Carr, "Manufacturing the Enemy," 52.

21. Auernheimer, "Der Kosovokonflict," 394.

22. Quoted in *Athens News,* May 9, 1999.

23. Quoted in ibid., Apr. 18, 1999.

24. Quoted in ibid., Apr. 25, 1999.

25. Quoted in ibid., May 6, 1999.

26. *Eleftherotypia,* Apr. 15, 1999.

27. Ibid., Apr. 6, 1999.

28. Christos Tellidis, "Ta Psemata enos Vromikou Polemou," *Klik,* May, 1999.

29. Takis Michas, "Ikones apo ena stratopedo," *Eleftherotypia,* June 3, 1999.

30. Quoted in *Eleftherotypia,* June 12, 1999.

31. Quoted in *Kathimerini,* Oct. 22, 1999.

32. Quoted in *To Vima,* Oct. 23, 1999.

33. Quoted in *Eleftherotypia,* Oct. 21, 1999.

34. Quoted in *To Vima,* July 11, 1999.

35. Andreas Papandreou, "I Kathodos tis Giougoslavias pros tin Kolasi," *Ta Nea,* June 17, 1993.

36. Simitis succeeded Papandreou as leader of the PASOK Party and as prime minister in 1996. He went on to defeat the ND Party in the 1996 and 2000 elections.

37. See chapter 6, "A Very Special Relationship."

38. Ibid.

39. Dr. Dušan Janić, taped interview with author, Athens, Apr., 2000.

40. Andreas Andrianopoulos "NATO's Odd Man Out," *WSJE*, Apr. 14, 1999. George Papandreou, son of Andreas Papandreou, was Greece's alternate foreign minister from 1996 until February, 1999, when he succeeded Theodoros Pangalos as foreign minister.

41. *Eleftherotypia*, Mar. 29, 1999.

42. Ibid., Apr. 28, 1999.

43. Ibid.

44. U.S. Department of State, "Patterns of Global Terrorism, 1999," http://www.fas.org/irp/threat/terror_99/europe.html.

45. Takis Michas, "A Death in Athens," *WSJE*, June 14, 2000.

46. November 17 is not the only terrorist group in Greece. Since 1975 there have been 146 terrorist attacks against U.S. targets in Greece, including rocket attacks and improvised explosives with incendiary devices. Only one of these cases, the one described herein, has been solved.

47. The inability to arrest the terrorists for some reflects the monumental incompetence of the Greek police and security forces. In one case, a crime scene was not sealed, and in this case policemen without gloves searched the general's bullet-riddled car, thus eliminating any hope of finding fingerprint evidence. In yet another killing, the police gave a spent bullet to a reporter as a "souvenir." Others attribute the failure to sympathies for the terrorists by unnamed members of the governing PASOK Party. In an interview published the same week in the Greek weekly *Pontiki*, former CIA chief James Wolsey stated that he believed that "there are people within the Greek government that know some members of November 17." The Greek government has flatly denied those allegations (Michas, "Death in Athens").

48. George Kassimeris, *Europe's Last Terrorists*.

49. The entire communiqué was published in *Eleftherotypia*, June 9, 2000.

Chapter 6. A Very Special Relationship

1. Leonidas Chatziprodromidis, *I Dolofonia tis Giougoslavias*, 295.

2. Ibid., 373.

3. Ibid., 372.

4. Quoted in *Eleftherotypia*, Jan. 25, 1996.

5. *Vreme*, Mar. 2, 1996.

6. *Independent* (UK), June 21, 1998.

7. For the Trepća story, see the International Crisis Group's report titled, "Trepća: Making Sense of a Labyrinth," Nov. 26, 1999.

8. *Business Week International*, June 28, 1999.

9. Quoted in *Financial Times* (UK), May 29, 1998.

10. Quoted in *Independent* (UK), June 21, 1998.

11. Chris Hedges, "Kosovo's Next Masters," *Foreign Affairs* 3 (May–June, 1999): 24–42.

12. Quoted in *Eleftherotypia*, Aug. 11, 1999.

13. Tim Judah, "How Milošević Hangs On," *New York Review of Books*, July 16, 1998, 46.

14. International Crisis Group, "Trepća," 7.

15. *Financial Times* (UK), June 10, 1997.

16. *Economist* (London), Mar. 14, 1998.

17. Saša Mirković, interview with author, Nov., 2000.

18. International Crisis Group, "Trepća," 6.

19. "Trepća management and workers call for a suspension of Serb-Greek deal," http://www.hology.com/mines/html.

20. The Greek government has never challenged the statements Mytilinaios made in the *Eleftherotypia* interview.

21. Takis Michas, "Milošević's Friends Inside NATO and the EU," *WSJE*, Oct. 13, 2000.

22. *Athens News,* Sept. 26, 2000.

23. Ibid.

24. *Athens News,* Sept. 27, 2000.

25. Quoted in *Eleftherotypia,* Sept. 26, 2000.

26. Quoted in ibid. It must be said here, however, that during the last year of the Milošević regime George Papandreou was in close contact with the Serb Democratic opposition and especially with President Koštunica, trying to help in the struggle for democratic reforms in the country. Most of the leading members of the Serb Democratic opposition have since recognized in public statements the positive role Papandreou and his adviser, Alex Rondos, played during the transition and the fact that his behavior differed radically from that of his predecessors, whose only contacts had been with the Milošević regime. However, most of Papandreou's activities in support of the Serb opposition were never publicized in Greece. That was because the dominant view both within his party as well as in Greece was that the changes taking place in Belgrade were "foreign instigated."

27. Quoted in ibid., Sept. 30, 2000.

28. Ibid., Oct. 2, 2000.

29. Quoted in ibid., Sept. 30, 2000.

30. Quoted in *Athens News,* Sept. 27, 2000.

31. *Rizospastis,* June 29, 2001.

32. *Eleftherotypia,* June 29, 20001.

33. See chapter 1.

Chapter 7. The Radicalization of the Orthodox Church

1. Clark, *Why Angels Fall.*

2. Quoted in *Eleftherotypia,* Dec. 5, 1995.

3. *Taftotita,* May 4, 2001.

4. *Eleftherotypia,* Sept. 17, 1994.

5. *Pliroforisi,* July–Aug., 1995. Also cited in *Anti,* July 3, 1998, 24. Archbishop Christodoulos, head of the Greek Orthodox Church, was bishop of the diocese at the time this editorial was published.

6. *To Vima,* Feb. 23, 1996.

7. *WSJE,* Sept. 9, 1998.

8. *Eleftherotypia,* Dec. 13, 1999.

9. For a comprehensive treatment of the problems religious minorities face in Greece, see Nikos Alivizatos, "The Constitutional Treatment of Religious Minorities in Greece," in *Mélanges en l'honneur de Nicolas Valticos,* ed. Renné-Jean Dubuy.

10. See Lipowatz, "Orthodoxos Christianismos."

11. *Eleftherotypia,* May 27, 1998.

12. Clark, *Why Angels Fall,* 148.

13. One such rift developed when the Greek government decided in June, 2000, to remove religious affiliation from state identity cards in order to bring the country in line with other members of the European Union. Hundreds of thousands of people gathered in demonstrations in Athens and Salonika carrying Greek and Byzantine flags and crucifixes. Teams of priests and nuns directed the demonstrators. The government sees this measure as protecting various religious minorities that exist in the country, whereas the church sees it as encroaching upon its powers and as an assault on Greek Orthodox identity. About 90 percent of the Greek population is Orthodox (*New York Times,* June 1, 2000). It is noteworthy that the archbishop of Greece later blamed the Jews for the identity card row: "You know who is behind the identity card issue? The Jews, and for the first time we have proof of that !" (quoted in *To Vima,* Mar. 15, 2001).

14. Andreas Papandreou, "Europe Turns Left," *New Perspectives Quarterly* 11, no. 1 (winter, 1994): 50.

15. Quoted in *Eleftherotypia,* Jan. 11 1992.

16. Ibid., Oct. 8, 1993.

17. Quoted in ibid., May 21, 1998.

18. *To Vima,* May 2, 1993.

19. Ramet, *Nihil Obstat,* 336.

20. Paschalis Kitromilides, "'Imagined Communities' and the Origins of the National Question in the Balkans," in *Nationalism and Nationality,* ed. Martin Blinkhorn and Thanos Veremis, 40; Dimitris Dimoulis, "'I Thriskeftiki Eleftheria os Kanonas Diaforopoiisis kai Ennoia Apokleismou," in *Nomika Zitimata Thriskeftikis Eterotitas stin Ellada,* ed. Dimitris Christopoulos, 142.

21. Alexander Shmeman, *I Apostoli tis Ekklisias sto Sichrono Kosmo,* trans. Iosif Roilidis, 131–43.

22. Adamantia Pollis, "Eastern Orthodoxy and Human Rights," 348.

23. Clark, *Why Angels Fall,* 171.

24. Quoted in *Eleftherotypia,* June 22, 2000.

25. Quoted in *New York Times,* June 1, 2000.

26. Quoted in *Eleftherotypia,* May 5, 1998.

27. Quoted in ibid., June 12, 1998.

28. Adamantia Pollis, "Greek National Identity: Religious Minorities, Rights, and European Norms," *Journal of Modern Greek Studies* 10 (1992): 179.

29. For the case of Serbia, see Ramet, *Nihil Obstat,* 175.

30. Helena Smith, "Clerics in Uniform," *Index on Censorship* 30, no. 2 (Mar.–Apr., 2001): 143.

31. *Eleftherotypia,* Dec. 7, 2000.

32. Ibid., Dec. 9, 1998.

Chapter 8. The Logic of Ethnic Nationalism

1. Quoted in ibid., Apr. 10, 1994.

2. The poll was taken during the period Apr. 2–15, 1999, and published in Vernardakis, ed., *I Koini Gnomi stin Ellada,* 81–113.

3. Breuilly, "Approaches to Nationalism," 165.

4. Adamantia Pollis, "Are There Human Rights in Ethnonational States?" (unpublished paper, 2000), 1.

5. Ibid., 19.

6. Eurobarometer study, Jan. 25, 2001.

7. Mazower, *Balkans,* 105.

8. Sugar, "External and Domestic Roots," 11.

9. See Anthony D. Smith, "The Ethnic Sources of Nationalism," in *Ethnic Conflict and International Security,* ed. Michael E. Brown, 28–37.

10. See Nikiforos P. Diamantouros, "Cultural Dualism and Political Change in Post-Authoritarian Greece" (Estudio/Working Paper, Centro de Estudioas Avanzados en Ciencias Sociales Instituto Juan March de Estudios e Investigaciones, Madrid, 1994).

11. Diamantouros and Larrabee, "Democratization in South-Eastern Europe," 33–34.

12. François Thual, *I Klironomia tou Byzantiou,* 21.

13. Mark Mazower, "High Political Stakes," *Index on Censorship* 30, no. 2 (Mar.-Apr., 2001): 135. On the minorities problem in Greece, see Hugh Poulton, *Balkans: Minorities and States in Conflict;* Panayotis Dimitras, "Minorites: Un plus ou un moins pour la Grece?" *L'Evenement Europeen* 16 (1991): 170–90; Christos Rozakis, "The International Protection of Minorities in Greece," in *Greece in a Changing Europe,* ed. Kevin Featherstone and Kostas Ifantis, 95–116; and Alexis Heraklides, "Mionotites kai Exoteriki Poltiki stin Ellada," in *To Mionotiko Phenomeno stin Ellada,* ed. Kostas Tsitselikis and Dimitris Christopoulos.

14. Pollis, "Greek National Identity," 179.

15. Dimoulis, "I Thriskeftiki Eleftheria," 89–90.

16. *I Thessalia,* Feb. 21, 1993.

17. Quoted in *Eleftherotypia,* Aug. 4, 1993.

18. Lambros Baltsiotis and Leonidas Embiricos, "Speaking in Tongues," *Index on Censorship* 30, no. 2 (Mar.–Apr., 2001): 145–48.

19. A more recent example is provided by the appeal in July, 1999, by three Turkish minority deputies, three Slav-Macedonian activists, and a number of NGOs for the recognition of a Macedonian and a Turkish minority. All of Greece's political parties denounced the appeal in the strongest of terms, as did twenty of the twenty-one national newspapers (the lone exception was the leftist daily *Avghi*). The act was seen as promoting "foreign interests," and those who signed the appeal were denounced as "Turkey's fifth column," "traitors," and as having "allegiance to foreign masters" (Panayotis Dimitras, "Anyone Who Feels Turkish," *Index on Censorship* 30, no. 2 [Mar.–Apr., 2001]: 152–53).

20. Quoted in ibid., 152.

21. Pollis, "Greek National Identity," 189.

22. Christopher Bennett describes this in *Yugoslavia's Bloody Collapse,* 219.

23. James Gow, *Triumph of the Lack of Will,* 78.

24. Constantine Mitsotakis, "Prologue," in Skilakakis, *Sto Onoma tis Makedonias,* 3. Skilakakis was Mitotakis's senior policy adviser from 1990–94.

25. Dimitris Christopoulos and Kostas Titselikis, eds., *KEMO—The Delphi Meetings: An Assessment*, 41-42.

26. Heraklides, "Mionotites ke exoteriki politiki," 234. See also Giannis Milios, "I Diamorfosi tou Neoellinikoy Ethnous ke Kratous os Diadikasia Ikonomikis ke Politismiakis Omogenopiisis," in *To Mionotiko Phenomeno stin Ellada,* ed. Kostas Tsitselikis and Dimitris Christopoulos, 281-315.

27. Mazower, "High Political Stakes," 135.

28. Ramet, *Social Currents in Eastern Europe,* 435.

29. Ramet, "Serbian Church," 102-103.

30. Quoted in *Eleftherotypia,* Oct. 15, 1997.

31. Ibid., Apr. 13, 1999.

32. Quoted in ibid., July 3, 1999.

33. Quoted in *WSJE,* Sept. 9, 1998.

34. Quoted in *Eleftherotypia,* Feb. 1, 1999.

35. See Diamantouros, "Cultural Dualism and Political Change"; and Heraklides, *I Ellada kai o "Ex anatolon Kindinos,"* 67-68.

Chapter 9. The New Anti-Americanism

1. *Eleftherotypia,* Dec. 7, 2000.

2. Examples of the "benign" anti-Americanism that flourished in Greece in the late 1960s and early 1970s are the early texts by Andreas Papandreou *(Democracy at Gunpoint* and *Paternalistic Capitalism)* and by sociologist Konstantinos Tsoukalas *(The Greek Tragedy).*

3. Nicolas Demertzis et al., "Media and Nationalism," *Journal of Press and Politics* 4, no. 3 (1999): 39-40.

4. In 1997, Orestis Kolozof, a member of the Politbureau and deputy of the Parliament, joined conservative and nationalist academics, politicians, and priests in signing a declaration opposing "U.S. dictated" negotiations between Greece and Turkey *(Ardin,* Nov., 1997).

5. *Rizospastis,* July 24, 1999.

6. Ibid., Dec. 10, 2000.

7. Ibid., Mar. 5, 2000.

8. Like, for example, the youth organization of the Political Spring Party created by former foreign minister Antonis Samaras.

9. *Rizospastis,* Dec. 24, 1995.

10. Ibid., Nov. 7, 2000.

11. Inteview with Politbureau member Orestis Kolozof in *Ethnos,* Feb. 13, 1994.

12. *Rizospastis,* Nov. 21, 2000.

13. *WSJE,* Dec. 18, 1999.

14. *New York Times,* June 14, 1992.

15. John Lukacs, *The End of the Twentieth Century and the End of the Modern Age;* Meštrović et al., *Road from Paradise.*

16. Nor is this an exclusive Greek phenomenon. When I interviewed French right-wing politician Jean Mari Lepen in Budapest a couple of years ago I was struck by the vehemence of his rejection of the American multiethnic model and the intensity of his fears that France and eventually Europe might "succumb" and adopt the U.S. model of societal pluralism *(Eleftherotypia,* Nov. 20, 1996).

17. "Implementing the American model in the Balkans," wrote conservative columnist Kostas Iordanidis, "means implementing 'democracy and tolerance of different ethnic and religious groups' in a new order. The fact that this model is capable of destabilizing specific state entities does not appear to bother Washington." *Kathimerini,* Nov. 15, 1999 (English language edition).

18. Huntington, *Clash of Civilizations,* 100. See chapters 1–4 of this book for more on the Bosnia issue.

19. These anti-Western attitudes were the result mainly of the following factors: The legacy of the Fourth Crusade and the sacking of Constantinople in 1204, Western missionary activities, and serfdom in areas occupied by the Venetians. See Steven Runciman, *Byzantine Civilization;* Philip Sherrard, *The Greek East and the Latin West;* Timothy Ware, *The Orthodox Church.*

20. Friedrich Engels and Karl Marx, *I Ellada I Tourkia kai to Anatoliko Zitima,* 287–88.

21. Clark, *Why Angels Fall,* 169.

22. Quoted in *New York Times,* June 25, 2000.

23. *To Vima,* Feb. 11, 2001.

24. Clark, *Why Angels Fall,* 197.

25. John Lester, "Overdosing on Nationalism: Gennadjii Zyuganov and the Communist Party of the Russian Federation," *New Left Review* 221 (1997): 42.

26. Christos Giannaras, "Thriskia kai Ellinikotita," in *Ellinismos kai Ellinikotita,* ed. Kostas Tsaousis; *I Neoelliniki Taftotita; Orthodoxia kai Disi sti Neoteri Ellada;* and *I Parakmi os Proklisi.*

27. James P. Piscatori, *Islam in a World of Nation-States,* 105–16.

28. Ian Lustick, *For the Land and the Lord.*

29. Quoted in *Athens News,* June 5, 1999.

30. *Eleftherotypia,* Dec. 4, 1994; quotation is in ibid., June 5, 1999.

Conclusion

1. Thanos Veremis, *Greece's Balkan Entanglement,* 68.

2. *Spectator* (UK), Nov. 12, 1993.

3. Ibid., Aug. 16, 1992.

4. *Times* (London), Dec. 18, 1993; ibid., Dec. 22, 1993.

5. *Sunday Telegraph* (London), Apr. 27, 1994.

6. Huntington, *Clash of Civilizations,* 78.

7. Takis Michas, *I Paremvoli ton Gallon Neon Philosophon.*

8. Todor Zhivkov was the Bulgarian head of state from 1971–89 when the country was ruled by a communist regime. He was arrested in September, 1992, and sentenced to seven years imprisonment for corruption, embezzlement, and abuse of power.

9. Cornelius Castoriadis, "Imaste Ipefthini gia tin Istoria mas," in *Tou Korneliou Kastoriadi,* ed. Teta Papdopoulou, 37–38.

10. Dimoulis, "I Thriskeftiki Eleftheria,"142–43.

11. Thual, *I Klironomia tou Byzantiou,* 74.

Bibliography

Almond, Mark. *Europe's Backyard War.* London: Mandarin, 1994.

Alivizatos, Nikos. "The Constitutional Treatment of Religious Minorities in Greece." In *Mélanges en l'Honneur de Nicolas Valticos,* ed. Renné-Jean Dubuy, 629–92. Paris: A Pedone, 1999.

Althusser, Louis. *Politics and History.* Trans. Ben Brewster. London: NLB, 1972.

Anderson, Benedict. *Imagined Communities: Reflections on the Origins and Spread of Nationalism.* London: Verso, 1996.

Andrianopoulos, Andreas. "NATO's Odd Man Out." *Wall Street Journal Europe,* April 14, 1999.

Antischolio. *Srebrenica.* Athens: Carthago, 1999.

Armenakis, Antonis, Theodoros Gotsopoulos, Nicolas Demertzis, Roe Panagiotopoulou, and Dimitrios Charalampis. "O Ethnikismos ston Elliniko Tipo: To Makdoniko Zitiima kata tin Periodo Dekembriou 1991–Apriliou 1993" ("Nationalism in the Greek Press: The Macedonian Issue during the Period December 1991–April 1993"). *Greek Review of Social Research,* January–August, 1996, 188–231.

Auernheimer, Gustav. "Der Kosovokonflict und die Griechishe Öffentlichkeit." *Südosteuropa* 48 (July-August, 1999): 389–401.

———. "Zum Bild der Turkei in Griechenland." *Südosteuropa* 48 (May–June, 1999): 336–58.

Babiniotis, Giorgos, ed. *I Glossa tis Makedonias* (*The Language of Macedonia*). Athens: Olkos, 1992.

Baltsiotis, Lambros, and Leonidas Embiricos. "Speaking in Tongues." *Index on Censorship* 4, no. 2 (2001): 145–51.

Banac, Ivo. *The National Question in Yugoslavia: Origins, History, Politics.* London: Cornell University Press, 1984.

Beaton, Roderick. "Romanticism in Greece." In *Romanticism in National Context,* ed. Roy Porter and Mikulas Teich, 92–108. Cambridge: Cambridge University Press, 1988.

Begzos, Marios P. *Orthodoxia I Misallodoxia?* (*Orthodoxy or Fanaticism?*). Athens: Parousia, 1996.

Bennett, Christopher. *Yugoslavia's Bloody Collapse: Causes, Course, and Consequences.* London: Hurst, 1995.

Berger, Peter, and Thomas Luckmann. *The Social Construction of Reality.* Garden City, N.Y.: Anchor Books, 1967.

Breuilly, Jean. "Approaches to Nationalism." In *Mapping the Nation,* ed. Gopal Balakrishnan, 146–74. London: Verso, 1996.

Brubaker, Roger. *Nationalism Reframed: Nationalism and the National Question in the New Europe.* Cambridge: Cambridge University Press, 1996.

Bryant, Christopher G. A. "Civic Nation, Civil Society, Civil Religion." In *Civil Society: Theory, History, Comparison,* ed. John A. Hall, 136–57. Cambridge: Polity Press, 1995.

Bureau of Democracy, Human Rights, and Labor. *Country Reports on Human Rights Practices for 1994.* Washington, D.C.: Department of State, 1995.

———. *Country Reports on Human Rights Practices for 1993.* Washington, D.C.: Department of State, 1994.

———. *Country Reports on Human Rights Practices for 1992.* Washington, D.C.: Department of State, 1993.

———. *Country Reports on Human Rights Practices 1991.* Washington, D.C.: Department of State, 1992.

Campbell, J., and Philip Sherrard. *Modern Greece.* London: Benn, 1968.

Center for Preventive Action. *Toward Comprehensive Peace in Southeast Europe.* New York: Twentieth Century Fund Press, 1996.

Chatziprodromidis, Leonidas. *I Dolofonia tis Giougoslavias* (*The Murder of Yugoslavia*). Thessaloniki: Paratitritis, 1999.

———. *Yugoslavia: I Ekrixi tou Ethnikismou* (*Yugoslavia: The Explosion of Nationalism*). Athens: Paraskinio, 1991.

Christopoulos, Dimitris. "Misleading Perceptions on Minority Rights in Greece." In *The New Millenium: Challenges and Strategies for a Globalizing World,* ed. Felicia Henel Krisna, 149–72. Aldershot: Ashgate, 2000.

———, and Kostas Tsitselikis. *KEMO—The Delphi Meetings: An Assessment.* Minority Group Research Center Study Series 4. Athens: Kritiki, 2000.

Clark, Victoria. *Why Angels Fall.* London: Macmillan, 2000.

Couloumbis, Theodoros, and Dalis Sotiris. *I Elliniki Exoteriki Politiki sto Katofli toy 21ou Aiona* (*Greece's Foreign Policy on the Eve of the 21st Century*). Athens: Papazisis, 1997.

Couloumbis, Theodoros, and Yannas Prodromos. "Greek Foreign Policy Priorities for the 1990s." In *Greece in a Changing Europe: Between European Integration and Balkan Disintegration?* ed. Kevin Featherstone and Ifantis Kostas. Manchester, UK: Manchester University Press, 1996.

Clogg, Richard. *A Concise History of Greece.* Cambridge: Cambridge University Press, 1992.

Crnobrnja, Mihailo. *The Yugoslav Drama.* London: I. B. Tauris, 1994.

Danforth, Loring. *The Macedonian Conflict.* Princeton, N.J.: Princeton University Press, 1995.

Dakin, Douglas. *The Greek Struggle in Macedonia, 1897–1913.* Thessaloniki: Institute for Balkan Studies, 1996.

Demertzis, Nicolas, Stylianos Papathanasopoulos, and Antonis Armenakis. "Media and Nationalism." *Journal of Press and Politics* 4, no. 3 (1999): 26–50.

Denying Ethnic Identity: The Macedonians of Greece. New York: Human Rights Watch, 1994.

Derrida, Jaques. *Of Grammatology.* Trans. Gayatri Chakvravorty Spivak. Baltimore: Johns Hopkins University Press, 1976.

Diamantouros, Nikiforos P. "Ellinismos kai Ellinikotita." In *Ellinismos kai Ellinikotita*, ed. D. Tsaousis. Athens: Estia, 1983.

———. "Cultural Dualism and Political Change in Post-Authoritarian Greece." Estudio/ Working Paper, Centro de Estudioas Avanzados en Ciencias Sociales Instituto Juan March de Estudios e Investigaciones, Madrid, 1994.

———, and Stephen E. Larrabee. "Democratization in South-Eastern Europe." In *Experimenting with Democracy*, ed. Geoffrey Pridham and Tom Gallagher, 24–64. London: Routledge, 2000.

Dimitras, Panayotis. "Anyone Who Feels Turkish." *Index on Censorship* 4, no. 2 (2001): 152–55.

———. "Minorites: Un plus ou un moins pour la Grece?" *L'Evenement Europeen* 16 (1991): 170–90.

Dimoulis, Dimitris. "I Thriskeftiki Eleftheria os Kanonas Diaforopoiisis kai Ennoia Apokleismou" ("Religious Freedom as Rule of Differentiation and Exclusion"). In *Nomika Zitimata Thriskeutikis Eterotitas stin Ellada* (*Legal Aspects of Religious Otherness in Greece*), ed. Dimitris Christopoulos, 81–165. Athens: Kritiki, 1999.

———. "I Nomiki Prostasia ton Ethnikon Mionotiton" ("The Legal Protection of National Minorities"). In *To Mionotiko Phenomeno stin Ellada* (*The Minorities Issue in Greece*), ed. Kostas Tsitselikis and Dimitris Christopoulos, 119–71. Athens: Kritiki, 1997.

Doubt, Keith. *Sociology after Bosnia and Kosovo*. London: Rowman and Littlefield, 2000.

Dragnitch, Alex. *Serbs and Croats: The Struggle in Yugoslavia*. New York: Harcourt, Brace, Jovanovitch, 1992.

Elefantis, Aggelos. "Apo tin Ethnikistiki Exarsi sto Perithorio" ("From Nationalist Extremism to Marginalization"). In *O Ianos tou Ethnikismou me i Elliniki Valkaniki Politiki* (*The Janus of Nationalism and Greek Balkan Policy*), ed. Aggelos Elefantis et al., 31–62. Athens: Politis, 1993.

Engels, Friedrich, and Karl Marx. *I Ellada I Tourkia kai to Anatoliko Zitima* (*Greece Turkey and the Eastern Question*). Trans. Panayotis Kondilis. Athens: Gnosi, 1985.

European Monitoring Center on Racism and Xenophobia. "EU Citizens: Cultural Diversity is a Strong Point." Press Release, January 25, 2001.

Fragoudaki, Anna, and Thalia Dragona, eds. *Ti ine I Patrida Mas? Ethnokentrismos stin Ekpaidevsi* (*What Is Our Country? Ethnocentrism in Education*). Alexandria: Athens, 1997.

Geerz, Cliford. *The Interpretation of Culture*. New York: Basic Books, 1973.

Gellner, Ernest. *Nationalism*. New York: Weidenfeld and Nicholson, 1997.

———. *Nations and Nationalism*. Oxford: Basil Blackwell, 1983.

Giannaras, Christos. *I Parakmi os Proklisi* (Decay as a Challenge). Athens: Nea Sinora, 1999.

———. *Orthodoxia kai Disi sti Neoteri Ellada* (*Orthodoxy and the West in Contemporary Greece*). Athens: Domos, 1992.

———. *I Neoelliniki Taftotita* (*Modern Greek Identity*). Athens: Grigoris, 1989.

———. "Thriskia ke Ellinikotita" ("Religion and Greekness"). In *Ellinismos ke Ellinikotita* (*Hellenism and Greekness*), ed. Kostas Tsaousis. Athens: Estia, 1983.

Gianoulopoulos, Gianis. *Exoteriki Politiki kai "Ethnika Themata" apo tin itta toy 1897 eos tin Mikrasiatiki Katastrophi.* (*Foreign Policy and "National Issues" from the Defeat of 1897 until the Asia Minor Catastrophe*). Athens: Vivliorama, 1999.

Glenny, Misha. *The Balkans, 1804–1999*. London: Granta Books, 1999.

Gounaris, Vasilis. "I Slavofonoi tis Makedonias" ("The Slavophones of Macedonia"). In *To Mionotiko Phenomeno stin Ellada* (*The Minorities Issue in Greece*), ed. Kostas Tsitselikis and Dimitris Christopoulos, 73–119. Athens: Kritiki, 1997.

Gow, James. *Triumph of the Lack of Will: International Diplomacy and the Yugoslav War.* London: Hurst, 1997.

———. "British Perspectives." In *International Perspectives on the Yugoslav Conflict,* ed. Alex Danchev and Thomas Halverson, 87–99. London: Macmillan, 1996.

Greece: Free Speech on Trial. Government Stifles Dissent on Macedonia. New York: Human Rights Watch, 1993.

Gutman, Roy. *A Witness to Genocide.* Shaftesbury: Element, 1993.

Hagen, William W. "The Balkan's Lethal Nationalisms." *Foreign Affairs* 78, no. 4 (1999): 52–65.

Halverson, Thomas. "The U.S. Perspective." In *International Perspectives on the Yugoslav Conflict,* ed. Alex Danchev and Thomas Halverson, 1–29. London: Macmillan, 1996.

Hedges, Chris. "Kosovo's Next Masters?" *Foreign Affairs* 78, no. 3 (1999): 24–42.

Heraklides, Alexis. *I Ellada kai o "Ex anatolon Kindinos"* (*Greece and "the Danger from the East"*). Athens: Polis, 2001.

———. *The Self-Determination of Minorities in International Politics.* London: Frank Cass, 1991.

———. "Mionotites ke Exoteriki Politiki stin Ellada" ("Minorities and Foreign Policy in Greece"). In *To Mionotiko Phenomeno stin Ellada* (*The Minorities Issue in Greece*), ed. Kostas Tsitselikis and Dimitris Christopoulos. Athens: Kritiki, 1997.

Herzfeld, Michael. *Anthropology Through the Looking Glass: Critical Ethnography in the Margins of Europe.* Cambridge: Cambridge University Press, 1987.

———. *Ours Once More: Folklore, Ideology, and the Making of Modern Greece.* Austin: University of Texas Press, 1982.

Hobsbawm, Eric. *Nations and Nationalism since 1780: Programme, Myth, Reality.* Cambridge: Cambridge University Press, 1990.

Honig, Jan Willem, and Norbert Both. *Srebrenica: Record of a War Crime.* Middlesex: Penguin, 1996.

Howard, Michael. "Diversity of Propaganda." *Index on Censorship* 4, no. 2 (2001): 156–60.

Huntington, Samuel P. *The Clash of Civilizations and the Remaking of World Order.* New York: Simon and Schuster, 1996.

Hutchinson, John. *Modern Nationalism.* London: Fontana Press, 1994.

Iliadakis, Manos M. *Apo to Makedoniko sti Nea Taxi kai sto Skopiano* (*From the Macedonian Issue to the New Order and the Skopjian Issue*). Athens: Papzisis, 1996.

Inalćik, Halil. *The Ottoman Empire: The Classical Age, 1300–1600.* London: Weidenfeld and Nicholson, 1973.

International Crisis Group. "Trepća: Making Sense of a Labyrinth." http://www.crisisweb.org/projects/sbalkans/reports/kos30rep.htm. Accessed November 26, 1999.

Jelavić, Barbara. *History of the Balkans.* 2 vols. Cambridge: Cambridge University Press, 1983.

Judah, Tim. *The Serbs: History, Myth, and the Destruction of Yugoslavia.* New Haven, Conn.: Yale University Press, 1997.

———. "How Milošević Hangs On." *New York Review of Books,* July 16, 1998.

Juergensmeyer, Mark. *The New Cold War? Religious Nationalism Confronts the Secular State.* Berkeley: University of California Press, 1993.

Kaplan, Robert D. *Balkan Ghosts.* New York: St. Martin's, 1993.

Karagiannis, Giorgos. *Eklissia kai Kratos* (*Church and State*). Athens: Pontiki, 1997.

Kassimeris, George. *Europe's Last Terrorists.* London: Hurst, 2001.

Kastoriadis, Kornelius. "Imaste Ipefuini gia tin Istoria mas" ("We Are Responsible for Our History"). In *Tou Korneliou Kastoriadi* (*Of Kornelius Kastoriadis*), ed. Teta Papadopoulou, 13–38. Athens: Polis, 2001.

Kitromilides, Paschalis. *Enlightenment, Nationalism, and Orthodoxy: Studies in the Culture and Political Thought of Southeastern Europe.* UK: Varioroum, 1994.

———. *The Enlightenment as Social Criticism: Iossipos Moisiodax and Greek Culture in the Eighteenth Century.* Princeton, N.J.: Princeton University Press, 1992.

———. "'Imagined Communities' and the Origins of the National Question in the Balkans." In *Nationalism and Nationality,* ed. Martin Blinkhorn and Thanos Veremis, 23–66. Athens: ELIAMEP, 1990.

Kofos, Evangelos. "National Heritage and National Identity in Nineteenth- and Twentieth-Century Macedonia." In *Nationalism and Nationality,* ed. Martin Blinkhorn and Thanos Veremis, 103–43. Athens: ELIAMEP, 1990.

———. "The Macedonian Question: The Politics of Mutation." *Balkan Studies* (1986): 157–72.

Kohn, Hans. *Age of Nationalism: The First Era of Global History.* New York: Harper, 1962.

Kollias, Aristidis. *I Ellada sti Pagida ton Servon* (*Greece in the Trap of the Serbs*). Athens: Thamiris, 1995.

Kostopoulos, Tasos. *I Apagorevmeni Glossa: Kratiki Katastoli ton Slavikon Dialekton stin Elliniki Makedonia* (*The Prohibited Language: State Repression of Slavic Dialects in Greek Macedonia*). Athens: Mavri Lista, 2000.

Lekkas, Pantelis. *I Ethnikistiki Ideologia* (*The Nationalist Ideology*). Athens: Katarti, 1996.

Lester, John. "Overdosing on Nationalism: Gennadjii Zyuganov and the Communist Party of the Russian Federation." *New Left Review* 221 (January–February, 1997): 34–52.

Liakos, Antonis. "Valkaniki Krisi ke Ethnikismos" ("The Balkan Crisis and Nationalism"). In *O Ianos tou Ethnikismou ke i Elliniki Valkaniki Politiki* (*The Janus of Nationalism and the Greek Balkan Policy*), ed. Aggelos Elefantis et al., 9–30. Athens: Politis, 1993.

Lipowatz, Thanos. "Die Trennung von Orthodoxer Kirche und Staat in Griechenland: Ein Immer Aktuelles Problem." *Südosteuropa* 47, no. 12 (December, 1998): 624–31.

———. "Orthodoxes Christentum und Nationalismus: Zwei Aspecte der Politishen Kultur Griechenlands in der Gegenwart." *Südosteuropa* 45, nos. 9–10 (September–October, 1996): 691–703.

———. "Orthodoxos Christianismos ke Ethnikismos: Dio Ptiches tis Synchronis Ellinikis Politikis Koultouras" ("Orthodox Christianity and Nationalism: Two Aspects of Contemporary Greek Political Culture"). *Hellenic Review of Political Science* 2 (1993): 31–48.

Lithoxoou, Dimitrios. *Mionotika Zitimata kai Ethniki Sinidisi sthn Ellada.* Athens: Leviathan, 1991.

Loizidis, Neophytos. "Greece and the Macedonian Problem after the Interim Accord of September 1995: In Search of a Solution to a Centuries Old Conflict." Ph.D. diss., Central European University, Budapest and Warsaw, 1998.

Lukacs, John. *The End of the Twentieth Century and the End of the Modern Age.* New York: Ticknor and Fields, 1992.

Lustick, Ian. *For the Land and the Lord: Jewish Fundamentalism in Israel.* New York: Council on Foreign Relations, 1988.

The Macedonian Affair: A Historical Review of the Attempts to Create a Counterfeit Nation. Athens: Institute of International Politics and Strategic Studies, 1992.

Makrides, Vasilios N. "Christian Orthodoxy versus Religion: Negative Critiques of Religion in Contemporary Greece." In *The Notion of "Religion" in Comparative Research,* ed. Uggo Bianchi, 471–79. Rome: "L Erma" di Bretschneider, 1994.

Malcolm, Noel. *Kosovo: A Short History.* London: Macmillan, 1998.

———. *Bosnia: A Short History.* London: Macmillan, 1994.

Mango, Cyril A. *Byzantium: The Empire of New Rome.* London: Weidenfeld and Nicholson, 1980.

Mavratsas, Kaisar. *Opsis tou Ellinikou Ethnikismou stin Kipro (Faces of Greek Nationalism in Cyprus).* Athens: Katarti, 1998.

———. "Cyprus Greek America and Greece. Comparative Issues in Rationalization, Embourgeoisement and the Modernization of Consciousness." *Modern Greek Studies Yearbook* (1995): 139–69.

Mazower, Mark. *The Balkans.* London: Weidenfeld and Nicholson, 2000.

———. *Inside Hitler's Greece.* New Haven, Conn.: Yale University Press, 1993.

———. "High Political Stakes." *Index on Censorship* 4, no. 2 (2001): 132–36.

Meštrović, Stjepan G. *The Balkanization of the West.* London: Routledge, 1994.

———, ed. *Genocide After Emotion: The Postemotional Balkan War.* London: Routledge, 1996.

———, Miroslav Goreta, and Slaven Letica. *The Road from Paradise: Prospects for Democracy in Eastern Europe.* Lexington: University Press of Kentucky, 1993.

Milios, Giannis. "I Diamorfosi tou Neoellinikoy Ethnous ke Kratous os Diadikasia Ikonomikis ke Politismiakis Omogenopiisis" ("The Formation of the Modern Greek Nation as a Process of Economic and Femographic Homogenization"). In *To Mionotiko Phenomeno stin Ellada (The Minorities Issue in Greece),* ed. Kostas Tsitselikis and Dimitris Christopoulos, 281–315. Athens: Kritiki, 1997.

Michas, Takis. *The Absence of Civil Society in Greece.* Aarhus, Denmark: Aarhus Universitet, 1989.

———. *I Paremvoli ton Gallon Neon Philosofon (The Intervention of the French New Philosophers).* Athens: Papazisis, 1984.

———. "Milosević's Friends Inside the EU and NATO." *Wall Street Journal Europe,* October 13, 2000.

———. "A Death in Athens." *Wall Street Journal Europe,* June 14, 2000.

———. "The New Anti-Americanism." *Wall Street Journal Europe,* December 28, 1999.

———. "Modern Orthodox." *New Republic,* December 13, 1999.

———. "Orthodox Church Strays into Political Field." *Wall Street Journal Europe,* September 9, 1999.

———. "Ikones apo Ena Stratopedo" ("Pictures from a Camp"). *Eleftherotypia,* June 3, 1999.

———. "Appeasing Criminals in Bosnia." *Wall Street Journal Europe,* September 24, 1997.

————. "Another Blow to Peace Prospects in Cyprus." *Wall Street Journal Europe,* January 8, 1997.

————. "Greece Questions the War Crimes Tribunal." *Wall Street Journal Europe,* August 9, 1996.

————. "How Athens Abets Bosnian Division." *Wall Street Journal Europe,* June 14, 1996.

————. "Greece Keeps Dismissing Serb Atrocities." *Wall Street Journal Europe,* August 22, 1995.

Mitsotakis, Constantine. "Prologue." In Theodore Skilakakis, *Sto Onoma tis Makedonias* (*In the Name of Macedonia*), 5–8. Athens: Elliniki Evroekdotiki, 1995.

Moustakis, Giorgos. *I Genisi toy Christianofasismoy stin Ellada* (*The Birth of Christian Fascism in Greece*). Athens: Kaktos, 1983.

Mouzelis, Nicos P. *O Ethnikismos stin Isteri Anaptiksi* (*Nationalism in Its Late Development*). Athens: Themelio, 1994.

————. *Politics in the Semi-Periphery: Early Parliamentarism and Late Industrialisation in the Balkans and South America.* London: Macmillan, 1986.

————. "Modernity Late Development and Civil Society." In *Civil Society: Theory, History, Comparison,* ed. John A. Hall, 224–49. Cambridge: Polity Press, 1995.

Nairn, Tom. *Faces of Nationalism: Janus Revisited.* London: Verso, 1997.

————. "Cyprus and the Theory of Nationalism." In *Small States in the Modern World,* ed. Peter Worsley and Paschalis Kitromilides. Nicosia, Cyprus: Zavallis Press, 1979.

Office of the Coordinator for Counterterrorism. *Patterns of Global Terrorism.* Washington, D.C.: Department of State, 2000.

Ostergaard, Uffe. *Tocqueville og de moderne analyser af den amerikanske nationalkarakter og politiske kultur.* Working Paper no. 18, Center for Kulturfoskning. Arhus, Denmark: Arhus Universitet, 1988.

Owen, David. *Balkan Odyssey.* London: Victor Gollancz, 1995.

Papadimitropoulos, Damianos. *I Ellada sti Valkaniki Krisi* (*Greece in the Balkan Crisis*). Athens: Polis, 1994.

Papakonstantinou, Michalis. *To Imerologio enos Politikou* (*The Diary of a Politician*). Athens: Estia, 1994.

Papandreou, Andreas. *Paternalistic Capitalism.* Minneapolis: University of Minnesota Press, 1972.

————. *Democracy at Gunpoint.* London: Deutsch, 1971.

————. *Man's Freedom.* New York: Columbia University Press, 1970.

————. "Europe Turns Left." *New Perspective Quarterly* 11, no. 1 (winter, 1994): 50–54.

————. "I Kathodos tis Giougoslavias pros tin Kolasi" ("The Descent of Yugoslavia to Hell"), *Ta Nea,* June 17, 1993.

Petropoulos, John. *Politics and Statecraft in the Kingdom of Greece, 1833–1844.* Princeton, N.J.: Princeton University Press, 1968.

Pettifer, James. *The Greeks.* London: Penguin, 1993.

Pipes, Daniel. *The Hidden Hand.* New York: St. Martins Griffin, 1996.

Piscatori, James P. *Islam in a World of Nation-States.* Cambridge: Cambridge University Press, 1986.

Pollis, Adamantia. *Kratos, Dikaio kai, Anthropina Dikaiomata stin Ellada* (*State, Law, and Human Rights in Greece*). Athens: Idrima Mesogiakon Spoudon, 1988.

———. "Ellada: Ena Provlimatiko Kosmiko Kratos" ("Greece: A Problematic Secular State"). In *Nomika Zitimata Thriskeutikis Eterotitas stin Ellada* (*Legal Aspects of Religious Otherness in Greece*), ed. Dimitris Christopoulos, 165–99. Athens: Kritiki, 1999.

———. "The Social Construction of Ethnicity and Nationality: The Case of Cyprus." *Nationalism and Ethnic Politics* 3, no. 1 (spring, 1996): 67–90.

———. "Eastern Orthodoxy and Human Rights." *Human Rights Quarterly* 15 (May, 1993): 339–56.

———. "Greek National Identity: Religious Minorities, Rights and European Norms." *Journal of Modern Greek Studies* 10 (October, 1992): 171–95.

———. "Notes on Nationalism and Human Rights in Greece." *Journal of Modern Hellenism* 4 (autumn, 1987): 147–60.

———. "Are There Human Rights in Ethnonational States?" Unpublished manuscript, 2000. Copy in author's possession.

Poulton, Hugh. *Balkans: Minorities and States in Conflict.* London: Minority Rights Publications, 1993.

———. *Who are the Macedonians?* Bloomington: Indiana University Press, 1995.

Ramet, Sabrina P. *Nihil Obstat: Religion, Politics, and Social Change in East-Central Europe and Russia.* Durham, N.C.: Duke University Press, 1998.

———. *Social Currents in Eastern Europe: The Sources and Consequences of the Great Transformation.* 2d ed. Durham, N.C.: Duke University Press, 1995.

———. "The Serbian Church and the Serbian Nation." In *Beyond Yugoslavia,* ed. Sabrina P. Ramet and Ljubiša S. Adamović, 101–23. Boulder, Colo.: Westview Press, 1995.

———. "The Macedonian Enigma." In *Beyond Yugoslavia,* ed. Sabrina P. Ramet and Ljubisa S. Adamovich, 211–37. Boulder, Colo.: Westview Press, 1995.

Reed, Fred A. *Salonica Terminus: Travels into the Balkan Nightmare.* Burnaby: Talon Books, 1996.

Report of the International Commission of the Balkans. *Unfinished Peace.* Washington D.C: Brookings Institute Press, 1996.

Report of the International Commission to Inquire into the Causes and Conduct of the Balkan Wars. 1914. Reprint, Washington, D.C.: Carnegie Endowment for International Peace, 1993.

Rozakis, Christos. *Politikes kai Nomikes Diastaseis tis Metavatikis Simfonias tis Neas Yorkis* (*Political and Legal Dimensions of the Transitional Agreement of New York*) Athens: I. Sideris, 1996.

———. "The International Protection of Minorities in Greece." In *Greece in a Changing Europe,* ed. Kevin Featherstone and Kostas Ifantis, 95–116. Manchester: Manchester University Press, 1996.

———. "Ta Adiexoda Stereotipa tis Ellinikis Exoterikis Poltikis" ("The Stalemate of Greek Foreign Policy"). In *Se Anazitisi Exoterikis Politikis.* Athens: Sinaspismos, 1996.

Runciman, Steven. *Byzantine Civilization.* Ohio: Meridian, 1970.

Sadkovich, James J. "The Response of American Media to Balkan Neonationalisms." In *Genocide After Emotion: The Postemotional Balkan War,* ed. Stjepan G. Meštrović, 113–57. London: Routledge, 1996.

Sarlis, Pavlos. *The Break-Up of Yugoslavia.* Athens: Papazisis, 2000.

Sherrard, Philip. *The Greek East and the Latin West: A Study in the Christian Tradition.* Limni, Evia: Denise Harvey, 1959.

Schmemann, Alexander. *I Apostoli tis Ekklisias sto Sichrono Kosmo.* Trans. Iosif Roilidis. Athens: Akrita, 1993.

Silber, Laura, and Allan Little. *Yugoslavia: Death of a Nation.* London: Penguin, 1995.

Skilakakis, Theodore. *Sto Onoma tis Makedonias* (*In the Name of Macedonia*). Athens: Elliniki Evroekdotiki, 1995.

Skopotea, Eli. *To "Protipo Vasilio" kai I Megali Idea: Opsis tou Ethnikou provlimatos stin Ellada, 1830–1880* (*The "Ideal Kingdom" and the Megali Idea: Aspects of the National Problem in Greece, 1830–1880*). Athens: Politipo, 1988.

Sluga, Glenda. "Identity Gender and the History of European Nations and Nationalism." *Nations and Nationalism* 4, no. 1 (1998): 87–111.

Sotirelis, George. "O Chorismos Kratous Ekklisias: I Anatheorisi pou den Egine." ("The Separation of Church and State: The Revision that Didn't Take Place"). In *Nomika Zitimata Thriskeutikis Eterotitas stin Ellada* (*Legal Aspects of Religious Otherness in Greece*), ed. Dimitris Christopoulos, 19–81. Athens: Kritiki, 1999.

Smith, Anthony D. *The Ethnic Origins of Nations.* Oxford: Blackwell, 1986.

———. *Theories of Nationalism.* New York: Holmes and Meier, 1983.

———. "The Ethnic Sources of Nationalism." In *Ethnic Conflict and International Security,* ed. Michael E. Brown, 27–42. Princeton, N.J.: Princeton University Press, 1993.

Smith, Helena. "Clerics in Uniform." *Index on Censorship* 4, no. 2 (2001): 141–44.

Stavros, Stephanos. "Citizenship and the Protection of Minorities." In Greece in a Changing Europe, ed. Kevin Featherstone and Kostas Ifantis, 117–28. (Manchester: Manchester University Press, 1996.

Stoianovich, Traian. *Balkan Worlds: The First and Last Europe.* New York: M. E. Sharpe, 1994.

———. *A Study in Balkan Civilization.* Toronto: Knopf, 1957.

Sugar, Peter F. "External and Domestic Roots of Eastern European Nationalism." In *Nationalism in Eastern Europe,* ed. Peter F. Sugar and Ivo J. Lederer, 3–54. 2d ed. Seattle: University of Washington Press, 1994.

Tarkas, Alexandros. *Athina-Skopje: Piso apo tis Klistes Portes* (*Athens-Skopje: Behind the Closed Doors*). Athens: Lavirinthos, 1995.

Tellidis, Christos. "Ta Psemata enos Vromikou Polemou" ("The lies of a Dirty War"). *Klik,* May, 1999, 148–52.

Thual, François. *I Klironomia tou Byzantiou* (*The Byzantine Inheritance*). Trans. Gianis Lampsas. Athens: Roes, 2000.

Tocqueville, Alexis de. *Democracy in America.* Vol. 1. 12th ed. New York: Knopf, 1984.

Todorova, Maria N. *Imagining the Balkans.* Oxford: Oxford University Press, 1997.

———. "The Balkans: From Discovery to Invention." *Slavic Review* 53, no. 2 (1994): 453–82.

Toynbee, Arnold. *The Western Question in Turkey and Greece: A Study in the Contact of Civilizations.* New York: H. Fertig, 1970.

Tsoukalas, Konstantinos. *Kratos, Kinonia, Ergasia sti Metapolemiki Ellada* (*State, Society, Labor in Postwar Greece*). Athens: Themelio, 1986.

———. *Exartisi ke Anaparagogi* (*Dependence and Reproduction*). Athens: Themelio, 1977.

———. *The Greek Tragedy.* London: Penguin, 1969.

———. "Ellin i Romios? Oi Antifasis tis Ethnikis mas Afigisis." ("Greek or Roman? The Contradictions of Our National Discourse"). *To Vima,* January 30, 1994.

Veremis, Thanos. *Greece's Balkan Entanglement*. Athens: ELIAMEP, 1995.

————. "From the National State to the Stateless Nation." In *Nationalism and Nationality*, ed. Martin Blinkhorn and Thanos Veremis, 9–22. Athens: ELIAMEP, 1990.

————, and Kouloumbis Thodoros. *Elliniki Exoteriki Poltiki: Prooptikes kai Provlimatismoi* (*Greece's Foreign Policy:Perspectives and Problems*). Athens: I. Sideris, 1994.

————, and Kofos Evangelos, eds. *Kosovo: Avoiding Another Balkan War*. Athens: ELIAMEP, 1998.

Vernardakis, Christoforos, ed. *I Koini Gnomi stin Ellada* (*Public Opinion in Greece*). Athens: Nea Sinora, 2001.

Vovou, Sisi, ed. *Vosnia-Erzegovini: I Machi gia tin Poliethniki Kinonia* (*Bosnia-Herzegovina: The Struggle for a Multiethnic Society*). Athens: Deltio Thielis, 1996.

Wallden, Sotiris. *Makedoniko kai Valkania, 1991–1994: I Adiexodi Poria tis Ellinikis Politikis* (*Macedonia and the Balkans: The Stalemate of Greece's Foreign Policy*). Athens: Themelio, 1994.

Ware, Timothy. *The Orthodox Church*. Rev. ed. London: Penguin Books, 1997.

Woodward, Suzan L. *Balkan Tragedy*. Washington, D.C.: Brookings Institution, 1995.

Zimmermann, Warren. *Origins of a Catastrophe: Yugoslavia and Its Destroyers—America's Last Ambassador Tells What Happened and Why*. Ed. Casey Mahaney. New York: Times Books, 1996.

Index

Photos are indicated with **bold** typeface.

TAKIS MICHAS has worked as a professional journalist since 1985. He is based in Athens, where he works for the Greek daily *Eleftherotypia.* He is the author of two previous books and has contributed articles to *The Wall Street Journal, The New Republic,* and other major publications. He was senior advisor on media to the Greek Minister of Trade and Industry and has done post-graduate studies at Arhus Universitet in Denmark, at the University of California in Santa Cruz, and at the International University in Dubrovnik.

Eastern European Studies

Stjepan G. Meštrović, Series Editor

Cigar, Norman. *Genocide in Bosnia: The Policy of "Ethnic Cleansing."* 1995.

Cohen, Philip J. *Serbia's Secret War: Propaganda and the Deceit of History.* 1996.

Gachechiladze, Revaz. *The New Georgia: Space, Society, Politics.* 1996.

Gibbs, Joseph. *Gorbachev's Glasnost: The Soviet Media in the First Phase of Perestroika.* 1999.

Knezys, Stasys, and Romanas Sedlickas. *The War in Chechnya.* 1999.

Lipták, Béla. *A Testament of Revolution.* 2001.

Meštrović, Stjepan G., ed. *The Conceit of Innocence: Losing the Conscience of the West in the War against Bosnia.* 1997.

Polokhalo, Volodymyr, ed. *The Political Analysis of Postcommunism: Understanding Postcommunist Ukraine.* 1997.

Quinn, Frederick. *Democracy at Dawn: Notes from Poland and Points East.* 1997.

Savage, Ania. *Return to Ukraine.* 2000.

Shlapentokh, Vladimir, Christopher Vanderpool, and Boris Doktorov, eds. *The New Elite in Post-Communist Eastern Europe.* 1999.

Tanovic-Miller, Naza. *Testimony of a Bosnian.* 2001.

Tasovac, Ivo. *American Foreign Policy and Yugoslavia, 1939–1941.* 1999.

Teglas, Csaba. *Budapest Exit: A Memoir of Fascism, Communism, and Freedom.* 1998.